The Frick Collection

2

Handbook of Paintings

D0033813

New York · 1985

Cover illustration: Johannes Vermeer, *Mistress and Maid* (detail)

Preface

This *Handbook of Paintings* is planned primarily for the use of
visitors while viewing the pictures in the galleries of
The Frick Collection. It is a new edition, substantially revised,
of the *Handbook* published in 1971. The text was compiled
from contributions made by past and present members of the
curatorial staff, assisted and edited by Joseph Focarino.
For more complete information on the paintings the reader is
referred to Volumes I and II of *The Frick Collection: An Illustrated Catalogue,* published in 1968. For brief room-by-room
commentaries on all the works normally found on exhibition,
including paintings, sculpture, and examples of the decorative
arts, see the *Guide to the Galleries* published in conjunction with
this *Handbook.*

Photography for the *Handbook* was the work of Richard
di Liberto and previous staff photographers. The book was
designed by Nathan Garland and printed by Conzett and
Huber AG, Zurich. Production costs were paid in part by the
Fellows of The Frick Collection.

Explanatory Note

Authorship: For the few paintings that cannot with certainty be attributed to specific artists, the following classifications are used: *Workshop of,* implying that the design may have been the master's but the execution was, in part at least, by an assistant; *Circle of,* implying that the unidentified artist probably had been trained by the master or influenced by close connection with him; and *Follower of,* implying that the unknown artist imitated the master's style but may have had no direct contact with him.

Dimensions: Measurements represent maximum stretcher or panel size. Height precedes width.

Date of acquisition: The date of each painting's acquisition is indicated by the first two digits of its accession number.

Location: Works of art in The Frick Collection are arranged with a freedom and flexibility that retain the atmosphere of a private house, and paintings may occasionally be relocated or removed from exhibition.

Historical Note

The Frick Collection was founded by Henry Clay Frick (1849-1919), the Pittsburgh coke and steel industrialist. At his death Mr. Frick bequeathed his New York residence and the most outstanding of his many art works to establish a public gallery for the purpose of "encouraging and developing the study of the fine arts." Chief among his bequests, which also included sculpture, drawings, prints, furniture, porcelains, enamels, rugs, and silver, were one hundred thirty-one paintings. Thirty-eight additional paintings have been purchased over the years by the Trustees from an endowment provided by the founder.

Mr. Frick grew up in the vicinity of Pittsburgh. From an early age he was interested in art, and his acquisitions recorded over a span of forty years show a continuing development of knowledge and discernment. After initially concentrating on Salon pictures and works by the Barbizon school, he purchased his first old masters around the turn of the century. In the next decade he acquired many of the distinguished paintings that established the character of the Collection as it is seen today. A more extended account of Mr. Frick's collecting is included in the biographical essay "Henry Clay Frick, Art Collector," which appears as an introduction to Volume I of *The Frick Collection: An Illustrated Catalogue*.

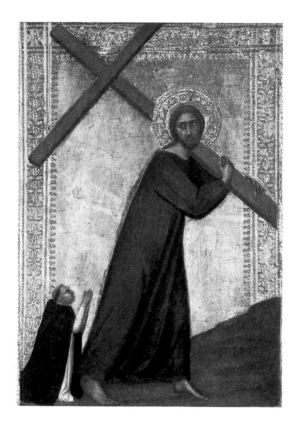

Barna da Siena Active around 1350

Though nothing certain is known of his life and even his name is in question, the master traditionally identified as Barna is firmly established on the basis of his frescoes in the Collegiata at San Gimignano as the leading Sienese painter in the years following the great plague of 1348.

Christ Bearing the Cross, with a Dominican Friar

Tempera, on poplar panel, 12 × 8½ in. (30.5 × 21.6 cm.). Painted about 1350–60. Acc. No. 27.1.1.

The attribution and dating of this remarkably affecting little panel are based on its close resemblance to the *Way to Calvary* fresco at San Gimignano. Unlike so many of Barna's contemporaries, the artist emphasizes Christ's sorrow rather than His physical pain. The diminutive Dominican monk kneeling at lower left is presumed to have commissioned the work, perhaps as a devotional image for his cell.

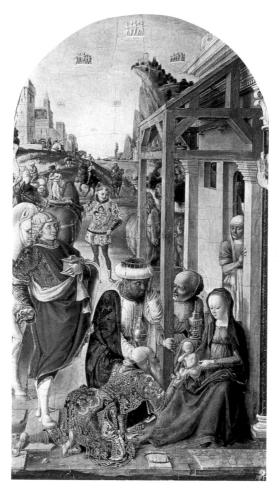

Lazzaro Bastiani d. 1512

Bastiani was born in Venice and achieved considerable prominence there. His rather conservative style is related to that of the Vivarini and to the work of Jacopo and Gentile Bellini.

Adoration of the Magi

Tempera, on poplar panel, 20½ × 11 in. (52 × 28 cm.).
Painted probably in the 1470s. Acc. No. 35.1.130.

During the fourteenth and fifteenth centuries the journey of the Magi to Bethlehem was commemorated by colorful processions with stops along the way to re-enact highlights of the voyage. Bastiani depicts the Adoration as though it were such a pageant, in which lavishly costumed performers and their exotic beasts wind through the landscape. The climax of the narrative takes place before the stable as the Magi pay homage to the King of Kings.

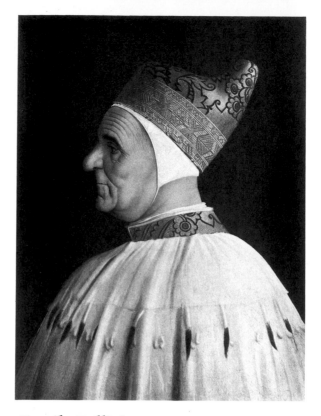

Gentile Bellini c. 1429–1507

Gentile and his brother Giovanni were trained in the studio of their father, Jacopo Bellini. As painter to the Republic of Venice, Gentile executed many official portraits and recorded in picturesque detail numerous pageants and ceremonies. In 1479–80 he was at the court of Sultan Mohammed II in Constantinople.

Doge Giovanni Mocenigo

Tempera, on poplar panel, 25½ × 18¾ in. (64.8 × 47.6 cm.). Painted probably between 1478 and 1485. Acc. No. 26.1.2.

Despite the fact that a late inscription on this panel (now painted over) identified the subject as the Doge Andrea Vendramin, it seems virtually certain that the painting actually represents Vendramin's successor, Giovanni Mocenigo (1408–85), who held various civil and military posts in Venice and its territories before being elected Doge in 1478. Mocenigo's features are recorded in several portraits preserved in Venice. The warm coloring and strong modeling of this work may reflect the influence of the artist's brother Giovanni.

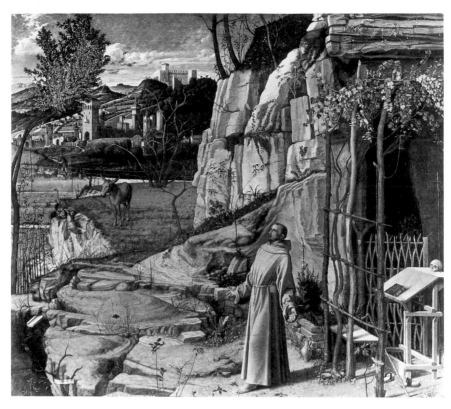

Giovanni Bellini c. 1430–1516

Giovanni Bellini began his career in the workshop of his father, Jacopo. In 1483 he succeeded his brother Gentile as painter to the Republic of Venice, and thereafter he was constantly employed by the State, as well as by Venetian churches and private patrons. He was one of the first Italian artists to master the oil technique of the northern European painters.

St. Francis in the Desert

Tempera and oil, on poplar panel, 49 × 55⅞ in. (124.4 × 141.9 cm.). Signed: IOANNES BELLINVS. Painted about 1480. Acc. No. 15.1.3.

St. Francis of Assisi (1181/82–1226), founder of the Franciscan order, is believed to have received the Stigmata—the wounds of Christ's Crucifixion—in 1224 during a retreat on Mount Alvernia in the Apennines. It is probably this event that Bellini has represented here through the naturalistic yet transcendental imagery of rays of light flooding the foreground from an unseen source at upper left. The artist has given special importance to the landscape setting, with its animals, plants, and rock formations that reflect the imagery of early Franciscan literature.

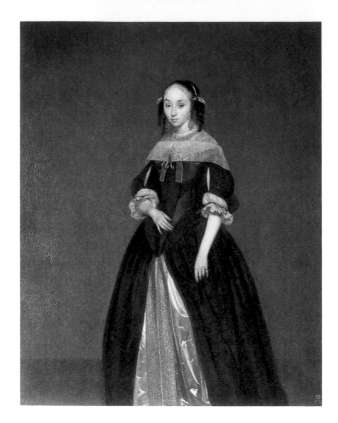

Gerard ter Borch 1617–1681

Ter Borch studied in his native Zwolle and then in Haarlem, where he painted the first of the genre scenes and portraits that made him famous. His extensive travels probably brought him to Spain, where he may have been influenced by Velázquez.

Portrait of a Young Lady

Oil, on canvas, 21⅛ × 16 in. (53.7 × 40.6 cm.).
Painted about 1665–70. Acc. No.03.1.113.

Small-scale portraits such as this were extremely popular in Holland during the second half of the seventeenth century. Characteristic of ter Borch's manner are the elegant proportions of the figure and the skillful depiction of light playing over rich fabrics. Substantially the same costume and pose are found in other portraits by ter Borch, suggesting that he painted from life only his subjects' heads and hands, adding costumes and backgrounds afterward.

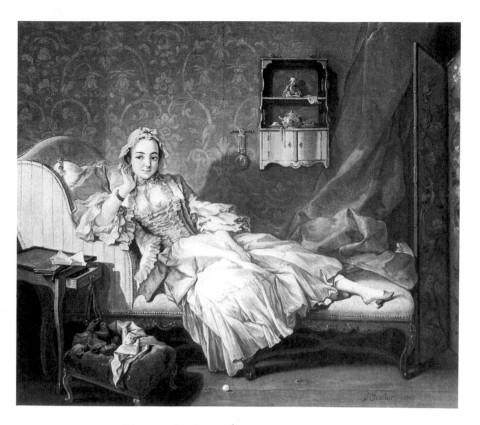

François Boucher 1703–1770

Born and trained in Paris, Boucher visited Italy in 1727–31, was elected to the Academy in 1734, and subsequently held high posts at both the Beauvais and Gobelins tapestry factories. Madame de Pompadour employed him for many commissions, and in 1765 he was named "Premier Peintre" to Louis XV. He had a great influence on the decorative arts of his day.

Madame Boucher

Oil, on canvas, 22 ½ × 26⅞ in. (57.2 × 68.3 cm.). Signed and dated: *f. Boucher. 1743.* Acc. No. 37.1.139.

When Marie-Jeanne Buseau posed for this informal portrait ten years after her marriage to Boucher, she was twenty-seven and the mother of three children. She frequently served as model for her husband, and in later life she painted miniature reproductions of his more popular pictures and made engravings after his drawings. The porcelain figurine and tea service on the étagère above her reflect Boucher's taste for the Oriental bric-a-brac so fashionable throughout the eighteenth century.

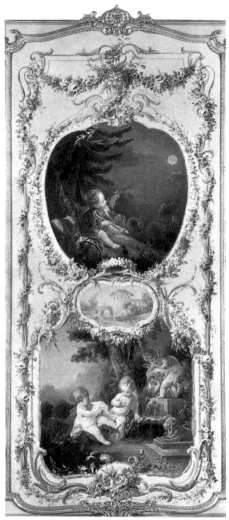 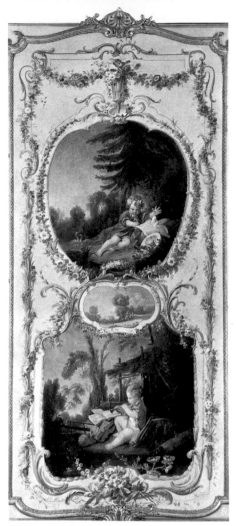

Astronomy and Hydraulics   *Poetry and Music*

Boucher

The Arts and Sciences
Oil, on canvas: Nos. 4, 5, 8, 9, 85½ × 38 in. (217.2 × 96.5 cm.);
Nos. 6, 7, 10, 11, 85½ × 30½ in. (217.2 × 77.5 cm.).
Painted probably between 1750 and 1753. Acc. Nos.
16.1.4–16.1.11.

According to tradition, Madame de Pompadour commissioned
these eight canvases for an octagonal room in the Château de
Crécy, an estate near Chartres that she bought in 1746
and redecorated extensively. The subjects of the panels, in
which children humorously mimic the occupations of adults,
probably allude to the Marquise's personal interests:

12

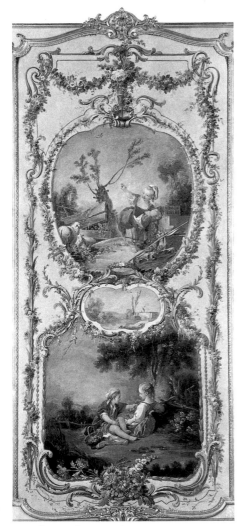

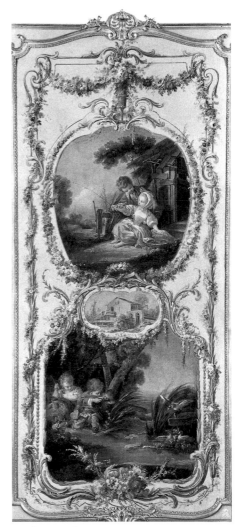

Fowling and Horticulture *Fishing and Hunting*

Architecture, Painting, and *Sculpture,* for example, recall her
enthusiastic patronage of those arts, *Hydraulics* was appropriate
to a château whose ingenious waterworks attracted wide
admiration, and *Chemistry* could well refer to the Marquise's
support of the Vincennes porcelain factory. The artist's wit is
particularly evident in such details as the exploding experiment
in *Chemistry* and the boy peering through the wrong end
of a telescope in *Astronomy.* The panels apparently remained
at Crécy until just before the destruction of the château in
1830. The overdoors with which they are now exhibited
are modern.

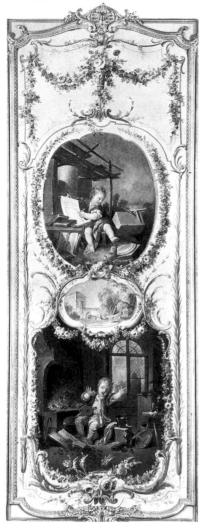 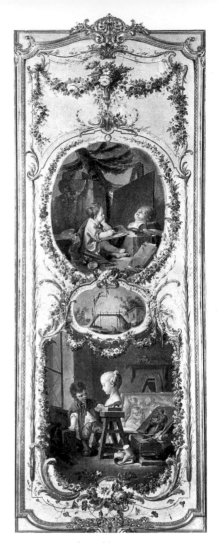

Architecture and Chemistry   *Painting and Sculpture*

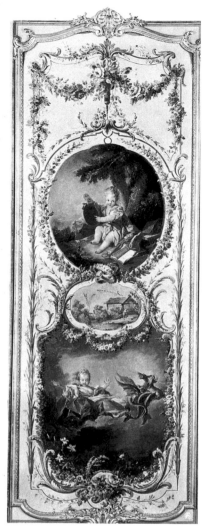 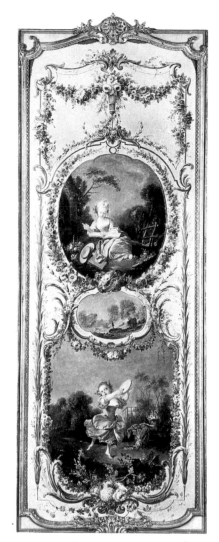

Comedy and Tragedy   *Singing and Dancing*

Spring

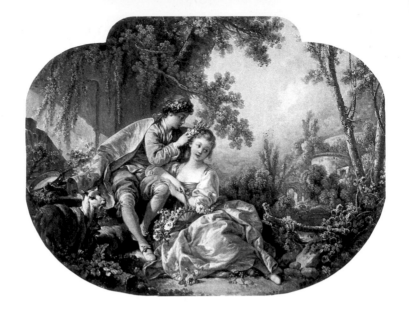

Summer

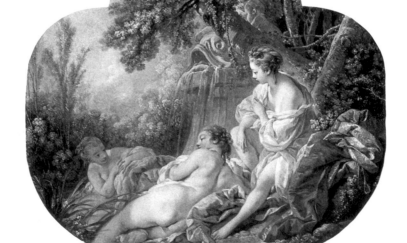

Boucher

The Four Seasons

Oil, on canvas, 22½ × 28¾ in. (57.2 × 73 cm.). Nos. 12, 14, 15, signed and dated: *f. Boucher 1755*. Acc. Nos. 16.1.12–16.1.15.

These four canvases, painted for Madame de Pompadour, probably were designed as overdoors for one of the Marquise's residences. Earlier representations of the seasons had usually depicted the labors performed at the various times of the year,

16

Autumn

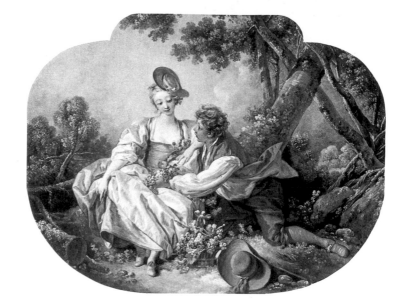

Winter

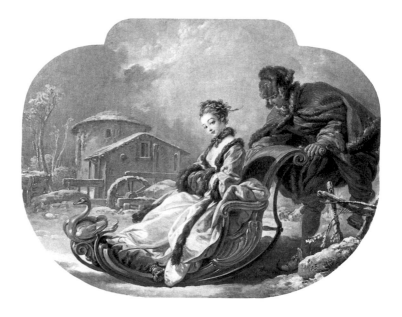

but Boucher characteristically chose to illustrate pleasant
pastimes instead, in the tradition of the *fêtes galantes* established
by his great predecessor Watteau. Attempts to identify the
lady in *Winter* as Madame de Pompadour and the central
bather in *Summer* as Louise O'Murphy, the King's mistress,
must remain inconclusive, as Boucher's women tend by the
1750s to fall into types, often resembling his wife.

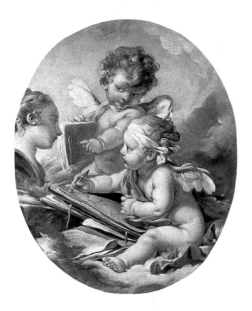 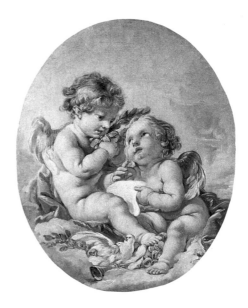

Boucher   **Drawing**   **Poetry**

Oil, on canvas, 15¾ × 12⅞ in. (40 × 32.7 cm.). Painted about
1760. Acc. Nos. 16.1.16 and 16.1.17.

Though companion pieces, these two works seem to have
been painted by different artists. *Drawing*, richer and warmer
in coloring, may be by Boucher himself. *Poetry*, which is
flatter in form and relies more on line than color and light for
modeling, is probably by an assistant.

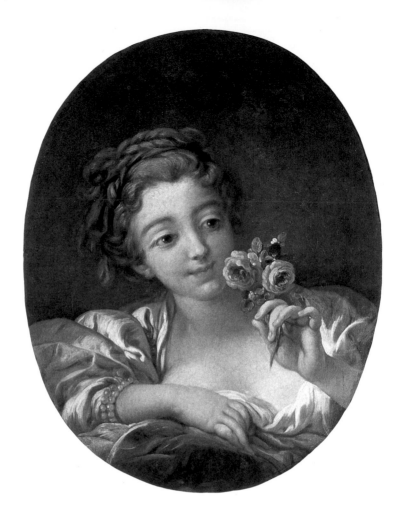

Boucher

Girl with Roses
Oil, on canvas, 21½ × 16¾ in. (54.6 × 42.5 cm.).
Painted probably in the 1760s. Acc. No. 16.1.18.

Elements of the pose and coiffure in this composition, which
perhaps was intended to represent the sense of smell, seem
to derive from certain paintings by Boucher representing
Vertumnus and Pomona, works that were reproduced in tapestry.

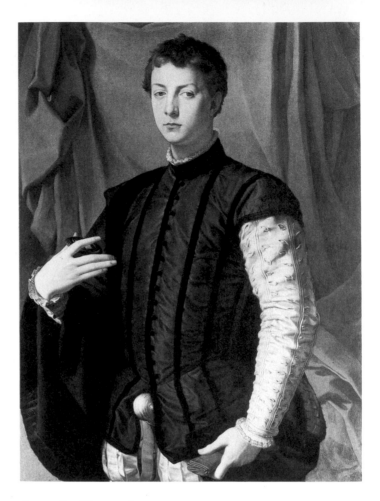

Agnolo Bronzino 1503-1572

*Agnolo di Cosimo di Mariano, called Bronzino, studied under
Pontormo and later collaborated with him. As court painter to Duke
Cosimo I de' Medici, Bronzino became the foremost portraitist of
Florence. He also executed religious and allegorical subjects as well
as decorations for Medici festivities.*

Lodovico Capponi

Oil, on poplar panel, 45⅞ × 33¾ in. (116.5 × 85.7 cm.).
Painted probably between 1550 and 1555. Acc. No. 15.1.19.

This elegant young aristocrat has been identified as Lodovico
Capponi (b. 1533), a page at the Medici court. As was his
custom, he wears black and white, his family's armorial
colors. His right index finger tantalizingly conceals the image
on the cameo he holds, revealing only the inscription SORTE
(fate or fortune)—an ingenious allusion to the obscurity of fate.

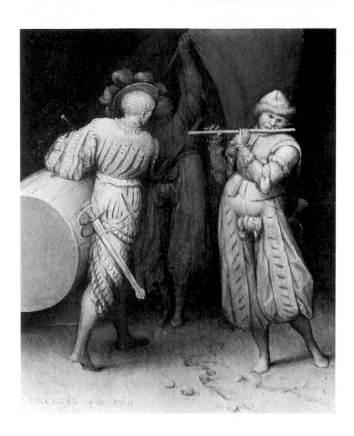

Pieter Bruegel the Elder Active 1551–1569

The earliest record of Bruegel is his entry into the Antwerp painters' guild in 1551. He traveled to Italy around 1552 and by 1555 was back in Antwerp, where he supplied the engraver Hieronymus Cock with designs in the style of Bosch. In 1563 he settled in Brussels. Bruegel's landscape paintings and peasant scenes had a powerful and lasting influence in the Netherlands.

The Three Soldiers

Oil, on oak panel, 8 × 7 in. (20.3 × 17.8 cm.). Signed and dated: BRVEGEL M.D.[L?]XVIII. Acc. No. 65.1.163.

This little panel, once in the collection of Charles I of England, represents a trio of *Landsknechte,* the mercenary foot soldiers who were a popular subject for printmakers in the sixteenth century. Bruegel may have executed it as a model for an engraving, though none is known, or simply as a cabinet piece. Lacking the lusty realism that characterizes his genre scenes, this work, along with a small number of other grisailles, perhaps reflects in its attenuated and elegant figures the influence of contemporary Italian painters.

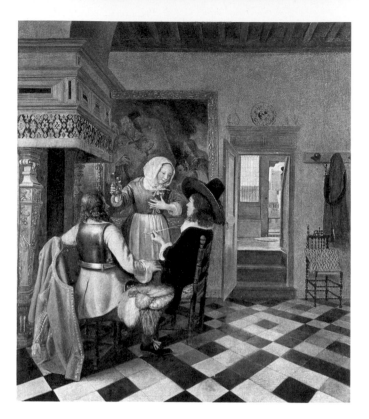

Hendrik van der Burgh, Attributed to
Active 1649–After 1669

Van der Burgh was enrolled as a foreigner in the painters' guild of Delft in 1649 and later worked in Leyden and Amsterdam. He painted chiefly interior scenes and was strongly influenced by Pieter de Hoogh.

Drinkers Before the Fireplace
Oil, on canvas, 30½ × 26⅛ in. (77.5 × 66.3 cm.). Painted perhaps in the 1660s. Acc. No. 18.1.78.

Both de Hoogh, to whom the present canvas was long attributed, and van der Burgh specialized in the depiction of intimate domestic scenes like this one. The same doorway, outer room, and distant houses appear in de Hoogh's *Duet* of 1670, but the figures and such distinctive features as the erratic perspective of the floor are more typical of van der Burgh.

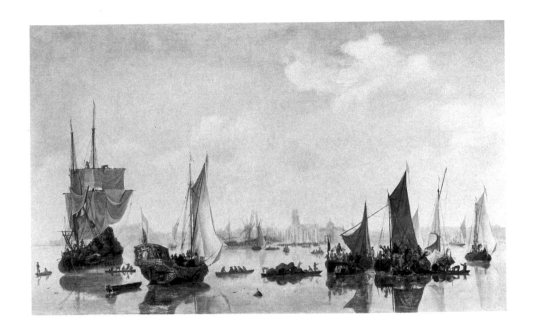

Jan van de Cappelle, Follower of

Van de Cappelle (c. 1624–79) was born in Amsterdam, where he painted seascapes and winter landscapes from about 1645 to the mid-1660s. His calm marine and river scenes inspired a number of imitators.

A View of the River Maas Before Rotterdam

Oil, on oak panel, 36½ × 61 in. (92.7 × 154.9 cm.). Acc. No. 06.1.20.

Among the landmarks identifying the city in the background as Rotterdam is the Gothic St. Laurenskerk, shown at center without the wooden steeple that was removed in 1645. This painting resembles in a general way the stately compositions of becalmed vessels that were a specialty of van de Cappelle, but the distant city view and other uncharacteristic elements suggest that it was done by a follower.

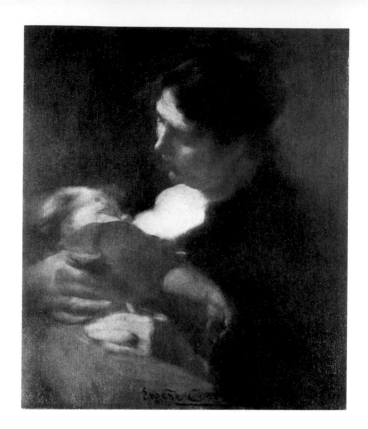

Eugène Carrière 1849–1906

Carrière worked as a lithographer in Strasbourg and a commercial
designer in Saint-Quentin before moving to Paris, where he studied
at the École des Beaux-Arts and subsequently under Cabanel. With
Rodin, Puvis de Chavannes, and others he founded in 1890 the Société
Nationale des Beaux-Arts, where he exhibited regularly.

Motherhood

Oil, on canvas, 22 × 18 ¼ in. (55.8 × 46.3 cm.).
Signed: *Eugène Carrière*. Painted probably in the 1880s.
Acc. No. 16.1.21.

Carrière painted many pictures on the theme of motherhood,
often using friends and relatives as models. His wife and one
of their numerous children are portrayed in the Frick canvas.
The vaporous browns and grays, typical of Carrière's work,
evoke the poetic imagery of the contemporary Symbolists, as
well as the sculptural style of Rodin.

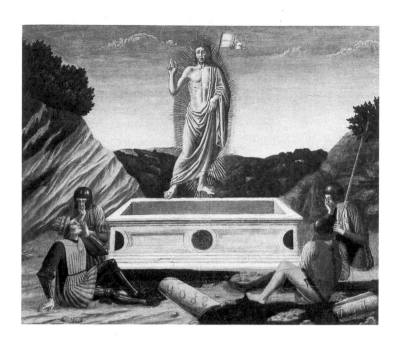

Andrea del Castagno, Attributed to
Before 1420–1457

Andrea di Bartolo di Simone, called Castagno after his birthplace
in Tuscany, worked primarily in Florence. One of the leading painters
of that city, he had many followers who explored various paths
suggested by his advanced style.

The Resurrection
Tempera, on poplar panel, 11 ¼ × 13 ¼ in. (28.5 × 33.7 cm.).
Acc. No. 39.1.143.

The austere dignity of the scene, with its simple composition,
gives this small panel an exceptional sense of monumentality.
In representing Christ as hovering in a *mandorla* above His
tomb, the artist follows a Florentine tradition of fusing the
events of the Resurrection and the Ascension. The painting
is thought to be one of a series of subsidiary panels from a now-
lost altarpiece executed perhaps by Castagno but more probably
by a follower, possibly Francesco Botticini (c. 1446–97).

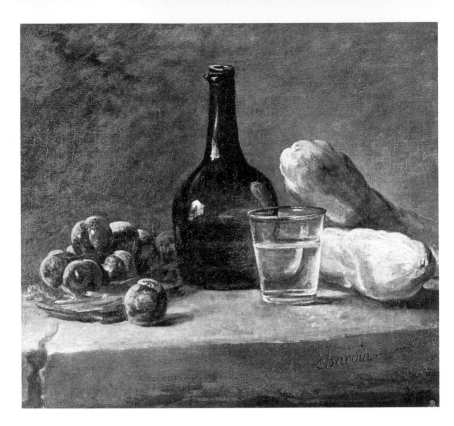

Jean-Baptiste-Siméon Chardin 1699–1779

Chardin, the son of a cabinetmaker, was born and trained in Paris. His official recognition began in 1728 with his admission to the Academy as a genre painter. Subsequently Louis XV awarded him commissions, a pension, and an apartment in the Louvre. Chardin's still lifes and middle-class domestic scenes were esteemed by contemporary collectors throughout Europe.

Still Life with Plums
Oil, on canvas, 17¾ × 19¾ in. (45.1 × 50.2 cm.).
Signed: *chardin*. Painted probably about 1730. Acc. No. 45.1.152.

Speaking of Chardin's still lifes, Diderot praised the "magic" of the artist's realism as well as his subtle color harmonies. Other contemporary critics admired Chardin's mastery of the varying effects of light on the surfaces of the familiar household objects with which he usually constructed his solidly designed compositions.

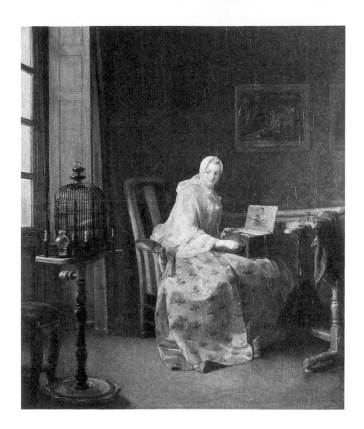

Chardin

Lady with a Bird-Organ
Oil, on canvas, 20 × 17 in. (50.8 × 43.2 cm.).
Painted in 1751(?). Acc. No. 26.1.22.

This characteristically unpretentious scene of everyday life
in a comfortable eighteenth-century household represents a
lady—possibly Madame Chardin—training a caged canary
to sing by playing an instrument known as a bird-organ. The
Frick canvas is one of several versions of a composition commissioned in 1751 by Louis XV.

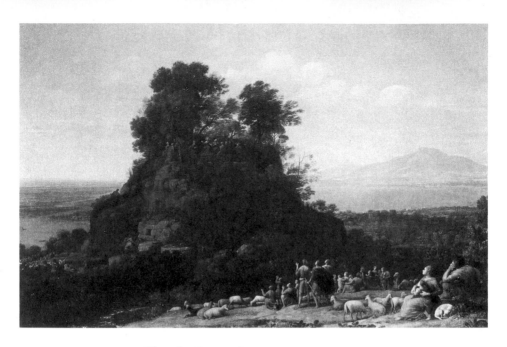

Claude Lorrain 1600–1682

*Claude Gellée, who was called Lorrain after his native province of
Lorraine, settled as a youth in Rome and spent nearly all his adult
life there. His early work was chiefly in fresco, of which little remains,
but his fame is based on landscape canvases. Patronized principally
by the Italian nobility, he also enjoyed an international reputation.*

The Sermon on the Mount
Oil, on canvas, 67½ × 102¼ in. (171.4 × 259.7 cm.).
Painted in 1656. Acc. No. 60.1.162.

Christ, surrounded by the Twelve Apostles, is shown preaching
to the multitude from the summit of Mount Tabor (Matthew
5:1–2). The artist has compressed the geography of the Holy
Land, placing on the right the distant Mount Lebanon and the
Sea of Galilee, with the towns of Tiberias and Nazareth on its
shores, and on the left the Dead Sea and the river Jordan.
The small foreground figures enhance the dramatic spatial
effects of the vast landscape. The painting was executed for
François Bosquet, Bishop of Montpellier, and later entered
the collection of William Beckford at Fonthill.

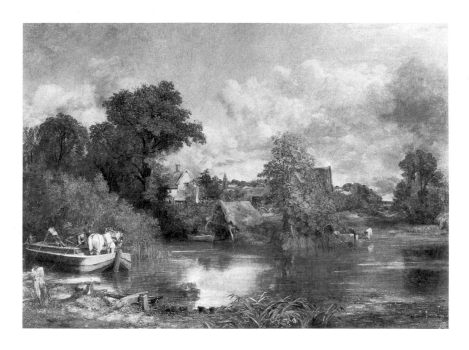

John Constable 1776–1837

Constable left his native Suffolk in 1799 to study at the Royal Academy, of which he became an associate in 1819 and a full member only in 1829. His landscapes, which depict chiefly the Suffolk countryside, had a deep influence on his contemporaries, particularly the French. His elaborately finished exhibition pieces were based on numerous sketches painted outdoors directly from nature.

The White Horse

Oil, on canvas, 51¾ × 74⅛ in. (131.4 × 188.3 cm.).
Signed and dated: *John Constable, A.R.A. | London F.1819.*
Acc. No.43.1.147.

The painting depicts a tow-horse being ferried across the river Stour in Suffolk at a point near Dedham where the tow-path switched banks. Constable, who described the scene as "a placid representation of a serene, grey morning, summer," went on in later years to comment: "There are generally in the life of an artist perhaps one, two or three pictures, on which hang more than usual interest—this is mine."

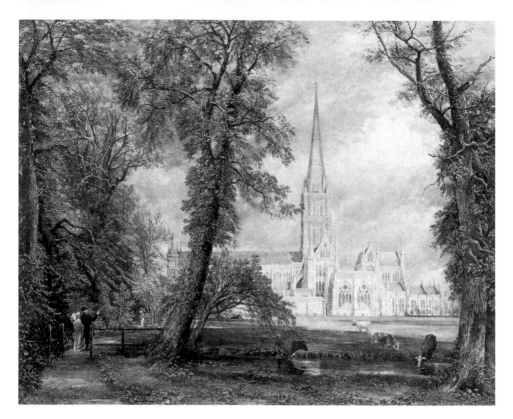

Constable

Salisbury Cathedral from the Bishop's Garden
Oil, on canvas, 35 × 44 ¼ in. (88.9 × 112.4 cm.).
Signed and dated: *John Constable. f. London. 1826.*
Acc. No. 08.1.23.

Constable painted several views of the south façade of Salisbury
Cathedral for his intimate friends Dr. John Fisher, Bishop of
Salisbury, and the Bishop's nephew Archdeacon John Fisher,
who had purchased *The White Horse* (see preceding entry)
in 1819. In this version two favorite subjects of nineteenth-
century artists—a medieval ecclesiastical monument and a
dramatic landscape—are particularly well united through the
arrangement of tree trunks and branches echoing the rising
lines of the cathedral spire.

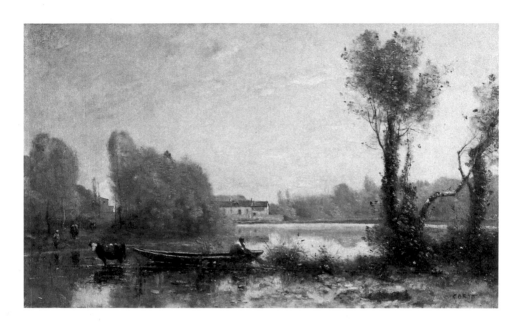

Jean-Baptiste-Camille Corot 1796–1875

Corot was born in Paris and studied there before leaving in 1825 for a three-year sojourn in Italy. After his return he worked in the Île-de-France and the Forest of Fontainebleau, and later in life he traveled and painted throughout much of France and elsewhere in Europe. He exhibited frequently in the Salons and won many honors.

Ville-d'Avray
Oil, on canvas, 17¼ × 29¼ in. (43.8 × 74.3 cm.).
Signed: COROT. Painted about 1860. Acc. No.98.1.27.

The large house at the center of this painting is probably the one Corot bought from the poet Estienne at Ville-d'Avray, a community west of Paris where his father also had a country house. The village and its pond recur frequently in the artist's work.

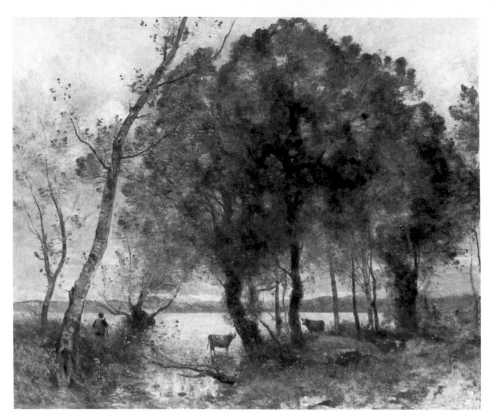

Corot

The Lake
Oil, on canvas, 52⅜ × 62 in. (133 × 157.5 cm.).
Signed: COROT. Painted in 1861. Acc. No.06.1.25.

Corot exhibited *The Lake* in the Salon of 1861. Though some
critics were beginning to question the artist's misty late
style—Thoré, for example, complained, "One is not sure where
one is and one has no idea where one is going"—others admired
the somber, nearly monochromatic coloring and broadly
massed design of this painting. One writer called it "a ravishing
landscape, simple in composition and full of grandeur."

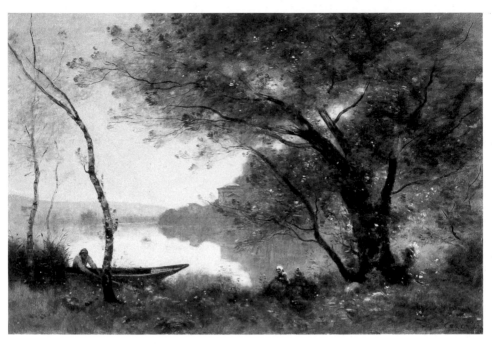

Corot   **The Boatman of Mortefontaine**
Oil, on canvas, 24 × 35⅜ in. (60.9 × 89.8 cm.).
Signed: COROT. Painted between 1865 and 1870.
Acc. No. 03.1.24.

Though inspired by the park of Mortefontaine outside Paris,
Corot's landscape is to a large degree imaginary. To enhance
the poetic mood of the scene he included on the far shore an
Italianate *tempietto,* which does not appear in his closely related
Souvenir de Mortefontaine of 1864 (Louvre).

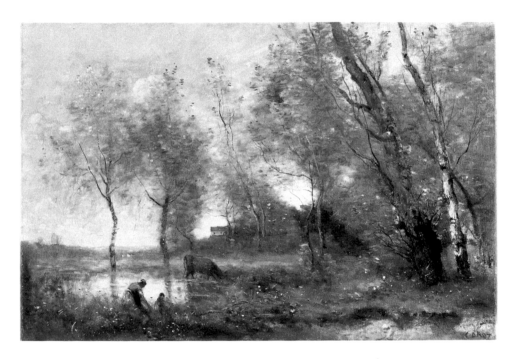

Corot

The Pond
Oil, on canvas, 19¼ × 29 in. (48.8 × 73.6 cm.).
Signed: COROT. Painted between 1868 and 1870.
Acc. No. 99.1.26.

This unlocated and probably imaginary landscape contains
elements found repeatedly in Corot's work, especially between
1860 and 1870: graceful stands of plume-like trees, waters
reflecting luminous skies, a few small figures, and cattle.

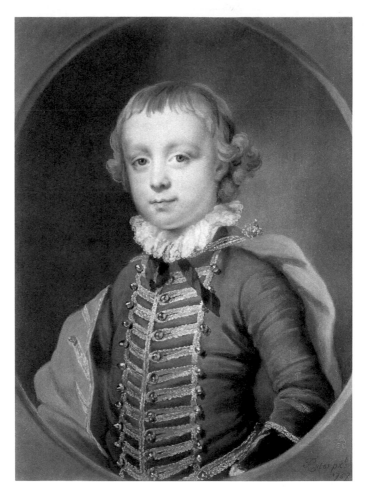

Francis Cotes 1726–1770

A native of London, Cotes was a portraitist known chiefly for pastels, though he also worked in oils. He was trained by Knapton, and his style shows the influence of such contemporary pastelists as Carriera, Liotard, and Latour. In 1768 he became a founding member of the Royal Academy.

Francis Vernon

Pastel, on paper affixed to canvas, 24 × 17⅞ in. (61 × 45.5 cm.). Signed and dated: *FCotes pxᵗ: 1757*. Acc. No. 15.1.137.

Done three years before the boy's death in 1760, this portrait shows Master Francis Vernon of Orwell Park, Suffolk, at the age of five. Through such works Cotes achieved considerable success with pastel portraiture in England at a time when the medium was more popular on the Continent.

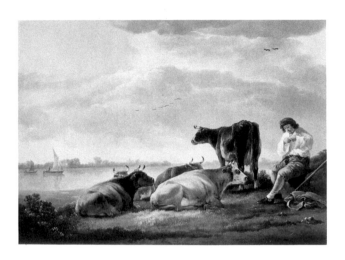

Aelbert Cuyp 1620–1691

Cuyp was born in Dordrecht and spent his entire life there. His early pictures recall those of his father, Jacob Gerritsz. Cuyp, and of Jan van Goyen. In the 1640s, under the influence of the Italianized landscapes of Jan Both and others, he developed the luminous style that characterizes his best-known works. He produced landscapes and occasional portraits until the mid-1660s, when he appears to have ceased painting.

Cows and Herdsman by a River

Oil, on oak panel, 19¾ × 29¼ in. (50.2 × 74.3 cm.).
Signed: *A. cuyp*. Painted probably in the 1650s.
Acc. No. 02.1.28.

The ruins on the horizon to the left of center may be those of the Huis te Merwede, a castle on the river Merwede a mile to the east of Dordrecht. Cuyp is celebrated for landscapes such as this which infuse realistic topography with an Arcadian spirit.

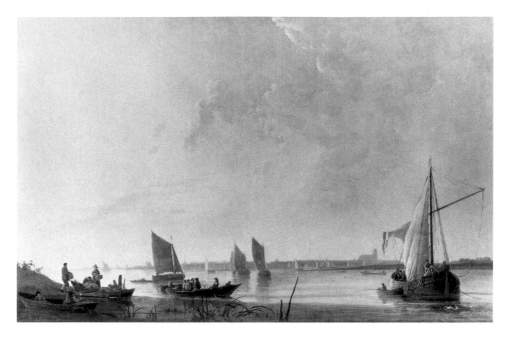

Cuyp

Dordrecht: Sunrise
Oil, on canvas, 40⅛ × 63⅜ in. (102 × 161 cm.).
Signed: *A. cuyp*. Painted about 1650. Acc. No.05.1.29.

This early morning scene, with its golden expanse of sky and water, is one of Cuyp's most ambitious attempts to render light and atmosphere. The painting may ultimately reflect the influence of Claude Lorrain, whose landscapes impressed many Dutch artists. Cuyp depicts Dordrecht as seen from the north, looking across the river Merwede. Most prominent among the recognizable buildings is the Groote Kerk, the church on the horizon to the left of the large boat in the foreground.

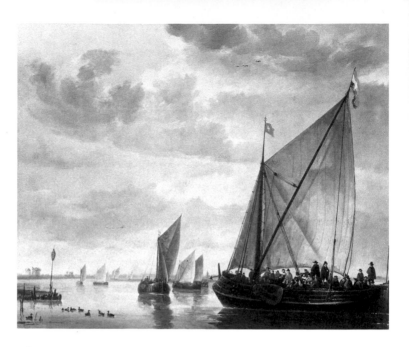

Cuyp

River Scene
Oil, on oak panel, 23 ⅛ × 29 ⅛ in. (58.7 × 74 cm.).
Signed: *A. cuyp.* Acc. No. 09.1.30.

Scenes of vessels plying the inland waterways around Dordrecht
were among Cuyp's specialties and permitted him to exploit
intricate effects of light, such as those on the sails in this panel.
Ferries of the type depicted in the right foreground were among
the chief means of public transportation in the Netherlands until
the expansion of stagecoach routes in the eighteenth century.

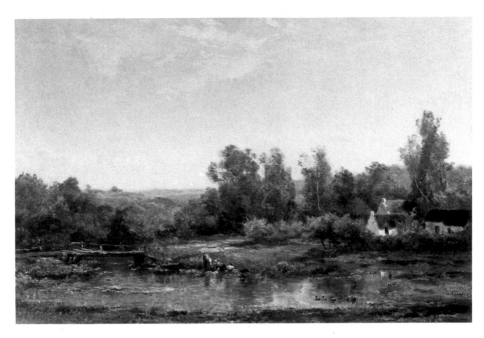

Charles-François Daubigny 1817–1878

*The son of a Paris landscape painter, Daubigny studied with Delaroche
and achieved his first great success when Napoleon III bought his
1853 Salon entry. Influenced by the Barbizon painters to work directly
from nature, he found many motifs for his landscapes in the countryside around Paris and during frequent trips through Brittany,
Normandy, and Picardy.*

The Washerwomen

Oil, on canvas, 20⅞ × 31½ in. (53 × 80 cm.).
Signed: *Daubigny*. Painted probably between 1870 and 1874.
Acc. No. 96.1.32.

The subject of women washing clothes by a stream is one
Daubigny repeated many times, often using sites along the
river Oise northwest of Paris. The present canvas, the earliest
of Mr. Frick's acquisitions bequeathed to the Collection, shows
in the sketchy brushwork of the landscape the influence of the
contemporary Impressionists.

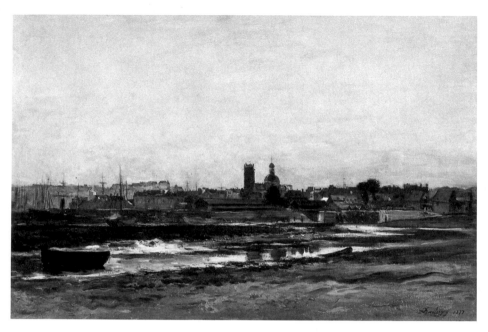

Daubigny

Dieppe
Oil, on canvas, 26⅜ × 39¾ in. (67 × 101 cm.).
Signed and dated: *Daubigny 1877*. Acc. No.04.1.31.

Unlike Turner, whose large view of Dieppe in The Frick
Collection records the picturesque bustle of that ancient Norman
port, Daubigny chose to depict the somber industrial side of
the city. The tower and cupola prominently silhouetted against
the sky in both paintings are those of the church of St.-Jacques.
The broad, vigorous application of paint in this canvas is
typical of Daubigny's last period and suggests affinities with
the early work of Manet and Cézanne.

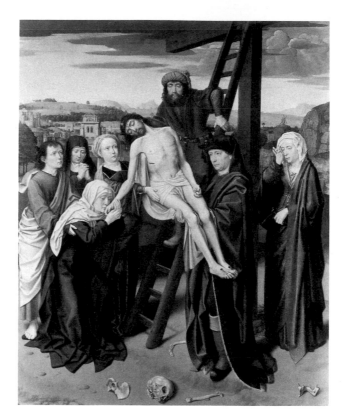

Gerard David Active 1484–1523

David was born at Oudewater, near Gouda. By 1484 he was in Bruges, where after the death of Memling in 1494 he became chief painter of the city. Documents show him working in Antwerp in 1515, but his death is recorded in Bruges.

The Deposition
Oil, on canvas, 56⅛ × 44¼ in. (142.5 × 112.4 cm.).
Painted about 1510–15. Acc. No. 15.1.33.

The somber dignity of the mourning figures and the austere simplicity of this composition greatly impressed David's contemporaries, who produced a number of copies and variants of *The Deposition*. This work is among the earliest extant northern European paintings executed on canvas in oil, rather than tempera, and is also one of the first in which the visual qualities of the oil medium are fully realized—most notably in the subtle ranges of the cold but vibrant tones and in the finely rendered details of the extensive landscape.

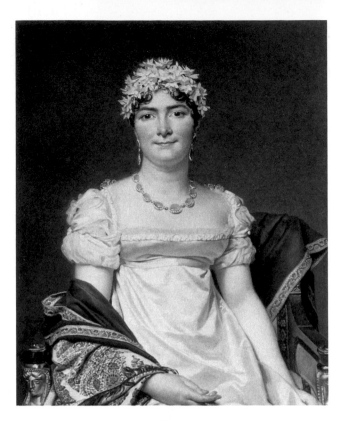

Jacques-Louis David 1748–1825

Born in Paris, David won the Prix de Rome in 1774 and the next year began a five-year residence in Italy. An ardent supporter of the Revolution and subsequently of Napoleon, he was a virtual dictator of the arts until the Emperor's downfall. Best known as a history painter, he also was extremely successful as a portraitist.

Comtesse Daru
Oil, on canvas, 32⅛ × 25⅝ in. (81.6 × 65.2 cm.).
Signed and dated: *L. David/1810.* Acc. No. 37.1.140.

In 1802 Alexandrine-Thérèse Nardot (d. 1815) married Pierre-Antoine-Noël Bruno, Comte Daru, who served as Secretary of State and Minister of War under Napoleon. David painted her portrait secretly as a surprise gift for the Count, who had helped him collect payment for *Le Sacre,* his vast painting of the coronation of Napoleon and Josephine. The writer Stendhal, who was in love with his cousin Daru's wife, recorded that David signed the finished work at four o'clock on March 14, 1810.

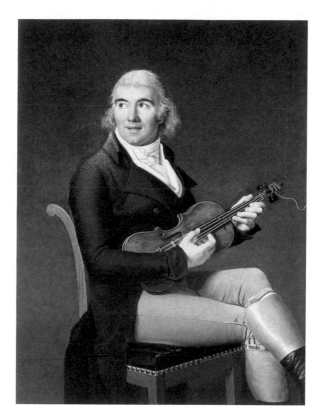

Césarine-Henriette-Flore Davin-Mirvault
1773–1844

Madame Davin-Mirvault, a native Parisian, was a pupil of David.
She exhibited paintings, mostly portraits, in the Salons and won
medals and considerable critical acclaim. During the Restoration
she ran a school for ladies which specialized in miniature painting.

Antonio Bartolomeo Bruni
Oil, on canvas, 50⅞ × 37¾ in. (129.2 × 95.9 cm.).
Painted probably in 1804. Acc. No. 52.1.160.

Composer, musician, and conductor, Antonio Bruni (1751–1821)
was born at Cuneo in Piedmont but spent much of his life in
Paris. During the Revolution he was an associate of David,
to whom this work once was attributed. Madame
Davin-Mirvault also knew Bruni, for he occasionally performed
at receptions in her house. The direct, lively personality
captured on this canvas, which was exhibited in the Salon of
1804, resembles that of the Comtesse Daru as recorded in
David's portrait of her.

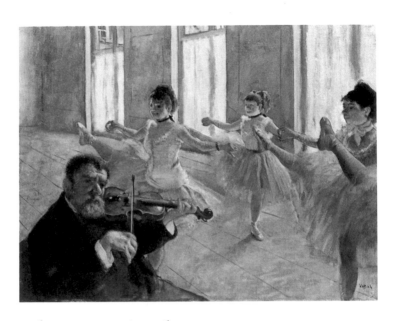

Hilaire-Germain-Edgar Degas 1834–1917

*Born in Paris, Degas studied at the École des Beaux-Arts and exhibited
at the Salons from 1865 until 1870. In 1872 he spent several months
in New Orleans, and later in life he traveled on the Continent,
in England, and in North Africa. His varied subjects, motifs drawn
largely from urban life, included dancers, working girls, women
bathing, and race horses.*

The Rehearsal

Oil, on canvas, 18¾ × 24 in. (47.6 × 60.9 cm.).
Signed: *Degas*. Painted probably in 1878 or early 1879.
Acc. No. 14.1.34.

In his choice of ballet subjects Degas generally avoided dramatic
moments of stage performance in favor of rehearsal scenes
such as this one, which is probably the *École de danse*
shown at the fourth exhibition of the Impressionists in 1879.
The blank, ordinary faces of the young dancers and their
conventionalized movements contrast poignantly with the
dark, brooding figure of the old violinist.

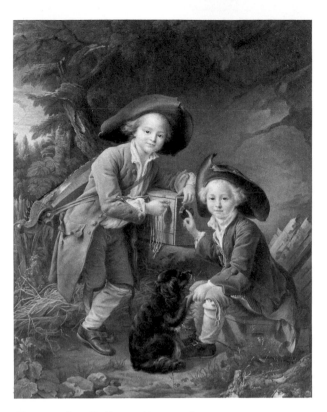

François-Hubert Drouais 1727–1775

Drouais was of Norman extraction but spent all his life in and around Paris. In 1757 he executed his first Royal commission, and the following year he was received as a full member in the Academy. Succeeding Latour and Nattier, Drouais became the most prominent French portraitist of the mid-eighteenth century, painting courtiers, foreign aristocrats, writers, and fellow artists.

The Comte and Chevalier de Choiseul as Savoyards
Oil, on canvas, 54⅞ × 42 in. (139.4 × 106.7 cm.).
Signed and dated: *Drouais le fils/1758*. Acc. No.66.1.164.

The standing boy with a hurdy-gurdy at his back is Marie-Gabriel-Florent-Auguste, Comte de Choiseul-Beaupré (1752–1817). Beside him, pointing to a peep-show box, sits his younger brother, Michel-Félix-Victor, Chevalier de Choiseul-Daillecourt (1754–1815). In costuming his subjects as Savoyards, the itinerants from Savoy who wandered over France working at odd jobs and in street fairs to support the families they left at home, Drouais probably intended to depict the brothers as models of filial devotion.

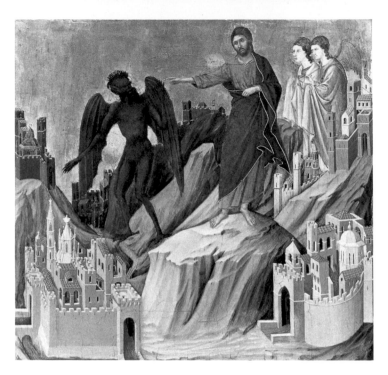

Duccio di Buoninsegna c. 1255–1319

Though Duccio was the leading Sienese master of his time, little is known of his life. He is first mentioned in a document of 1278, and in 1285 he received a commission for a painting assumed to be the Rucellai Madonna *now in the Uffizi. His greatest work is the* Maestà, *a huge altarpiece commissioned in 1308 and carried to the Duomo of Siena in solemn procession on June 9, 1311.*

The Temptation of Christ on the Mountain

Tempera, on poplar panel, 17 × 18 ⅛ in. (43.2 × 46 cm.).
Painted between 1308 and 1311. Acc. No. 27.1.35.

Christ is shown rejecting the devil, who offers Him "all the kingdoms of the world" if He will worship him (Matthew 4:8–11). Duccio retains medieval conventions in representing the figures as large and the spurned kingdoms as small, thus suggesting a scale of relative values rather than naturalistic proportions. This panel is one of a series of scenes from the life of Christ painted on the reverse of Duccio's *Maestà*.

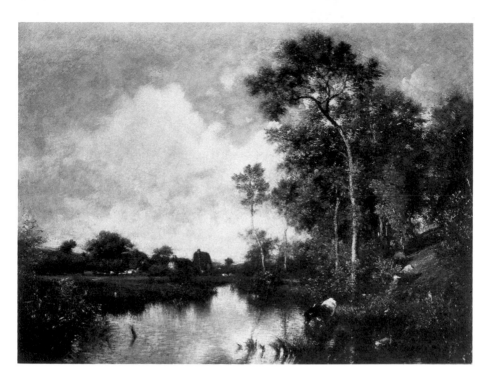

Jules Dupré 1811–1889

Dupré was born in Nantes and went to Paris around 1832. He exhibited in the Salons and associated with painters of the Barbizon group, including Rousseau, Troyon, and Daubigny.

The River

Oil, on canvas, 17 × 23 in. (43.2 × 58.4 cm.). Acc. No. 97.1.36.

During a visit to England in 1834 Dupré met Constable, whose work strongly affected his style. The influence of the older painter's oil sketches is evident in this canvas, where short, broken brushstrokes are skillfully employed to capture evanescent effects of light and atmosphere.

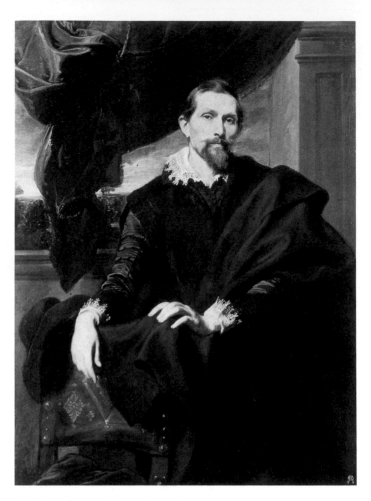

Sir Anthony Van Dyck 1599–1641

*Van Dyck was a native of Antwerp, where he was apprenticed to
Hendrik van Balen and later served as Rubens' chief assistant.
He visited London in 1620 and worked in Italy from 1621 until 1627,
when he returned to Antwerp. From 1632 until his death he was
active chiefly in England.*

Frans Snyders
Oil, on canvas, 56⅛ × 41½ in. (142.5 × 105.4 cm.).
Painted about 1620. Acc. No. 09.1.39.

Frans Snyders (1579–1657) was a celebrated and prolific painter
of still lifes, animals, and hunting scenes, and often assisted
Rubens in those capacities. He was an intimate friend of
Van Dyck, who also depicted him in an etching. This painting
and its pendant of Margareta Snyders are much closer to
Rubens' style than the works of Van Dyck's later English period.

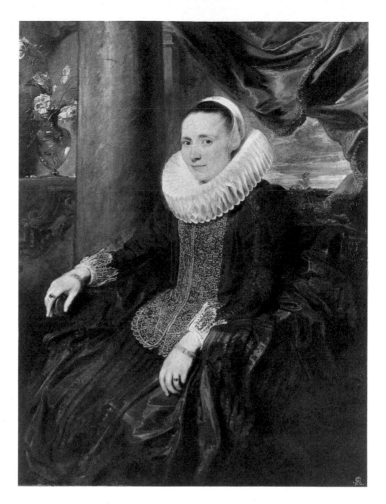

Van Dyck

Margareta Snyders
Oil, on canvas, 51½ × 39⅛ in. (130.7 × 99.3 cm.).
Painted about 1620. Acc. No. 09.1.42.

Margareta de Vos was a sister of the Antwerp painters Cornelis
and Paul de Vos, both of whom occasionally worked for
Rubens. She married Frans Snyders in 1611. Recognizable
among the blossoms at upper left in her portrait are a
daffodil, a poet's narcissus, and poppies, all flowers sacred
to Ceres or her daughter Proserpina and symbolic of sorrow
and death. Their presence here suggests that the couple may
have been in mourning, possibly for a young daughter.

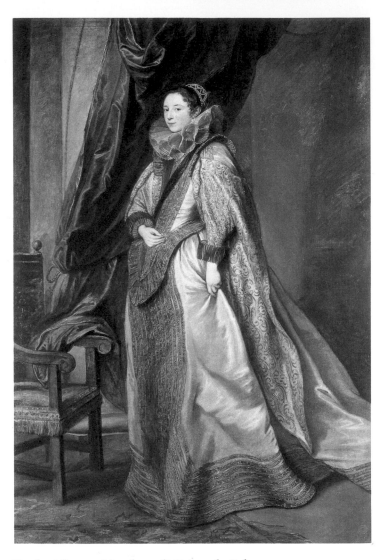

Van Dyck

Paola Adorno, Marchesa di Brignole Sale
Oil, on canvas, 90⅞ × 61⅝ in. (230.8 × 156.5 cm.).
Painted between 1622 and 1627. Acc. No. 14.1.43.

Paola Adorno, member of one of the most distinguished
Genoese families, married Anton Giulio Brignole, a poet,
writer, and political figure who entered the priesthood after
her death in 1648. Van Dyck portrayed her at least three times
during his stay in Genoa, and also painted her husband and
young son. The elegantly elongated proportions he used in
portraits such as this one came to typify his later style.

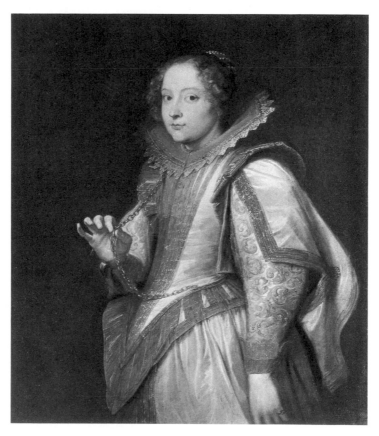

Van Dyck

Marchesa Giovanna Cattaneo

Oil, on canvas, 40⅜ × 34 in. (102.6 × 86.4 cm.).
Painted between 1622 and 1627. Acc. No.07.1.41.

Giovanna Battista Cattaneo, traditionally identified as the
subject of this portrait, belonged to a Genoese family that
included doges, cardinals, scholars, and statesmen. The heavy
gold chain *(catena)* she so conspicuously displays probably is
a play on her family name, which may also be reflected in
the c-shaped scrolls embroidered on her sleeves. The abrupt
termination of the figure suggests that the portrait has been
cut down from a larger size.

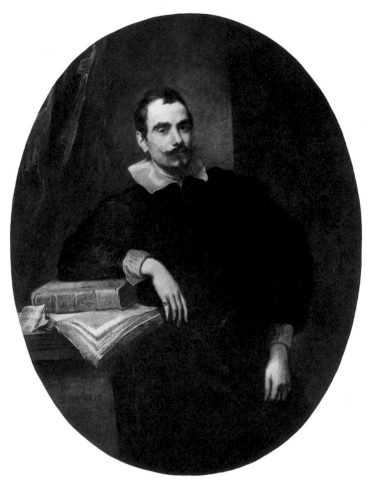

Van Dyck

Ottaviano Canevari
Oil, on canvas, 51 ¼ × 39 in. (130.2 × 99.1 cm.).
Painted probably in 1627. Acc. No.05.1.38.

Ottaviano Canevari was a Genoese magistrate and Senator
and the brother of Demetrio Canevari, a celebrated physician,
writer, and bibliophile who was thought to be the subject of
this portrait until cleaning uncovered Ottaviano's name on
the letter at left. When Demetrio died in 1625 he bequeathed
in trust a vast library and named Ottaviano as executor, which
may explain why Van Dyck included in the painting volumes
by Hippocrates and Aristotle.

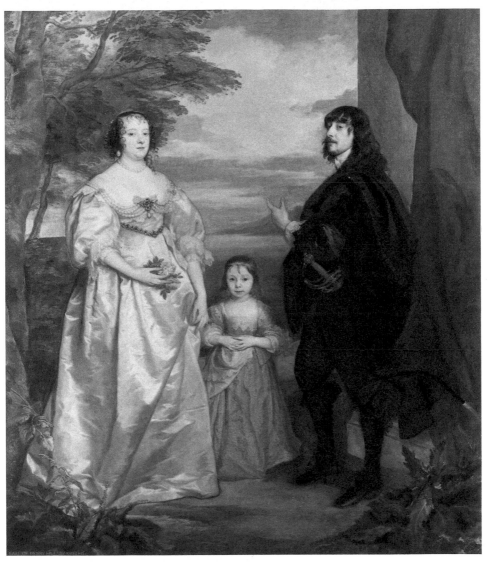

Van Dyck **James, Seventh Earl of Derby, His Lady and Child**
Oil, on canvas, 97 × 84⅛ in. (246.4 × 213.7 cm.).
Painted between 1632 and 1641. Acc. No. 13.1.40.

This imposing work, typical of the large group portraits
Van Dyck painted during his last English period, represents
James Stanley, seventh Earl of Derby, with his wife Charlotte
de la Trémoille and one of their daughters. The Earl was a
writer of history and devotional works as well as a Royalist
commander at the time of the Civil War. He was captured and
executed by Commonwealth forces in 1651. During the war
his wife became famous for her spirited defense of Lathom
House, the Derby's country seat.

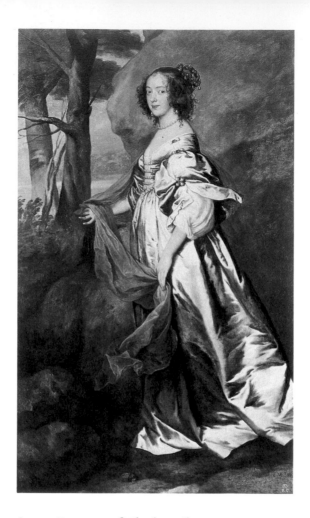

Van Dyck

Anne, Countess of Clanbrassil
Oil, on canvas, 83½ × 50¼ in. (212.1 × 127.6 cm.).
Painted probably in 1636. Acc. No. 17.1.37.

Lady Anne Carey (d. 1689), daughter of the second Earl of
Monmouth, was married in 1635 to James Hamilton, second
Viscount Claneboye, later Earl of Clanbrassil. An old source
describes Lady Anne as "very handsome, and witty . . . a woman
extraordinary in knowledge, virtue, and piety." A similar
background, which must have been a studio property, appears
in Van Dyck's portrait of the Countess' aunt and in one of the
first Duke of Hamilton.

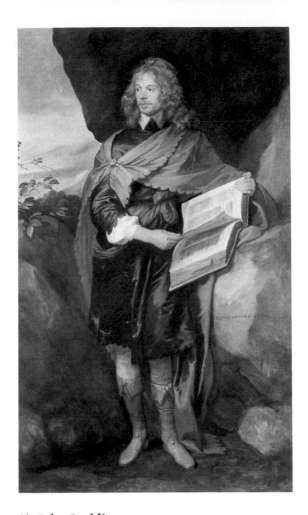

Van Dyck

Sir John Suckling
Oil, on canvas, 85 ¼ × 51 ¼ in. (216.5 × 130.2 cm.).
Painted between 1632 and 1641. Acc. No. 18.1.44.

In his own day John Suckling (1609–42) was famous not only
as a lyric poet, but also as a wit, gambler, soldier, and gallant
who conducted himself with an extravagance remarkable
even at the court of Charles I. Implicated in a plot to put
Charles in command of the army, which was then loyal to
the Roundheads, he fled in 1641 to Paris, where he later
reputedly committed suicide. In this portrait Suckling holds
a volume of Shakespeare opened to *Hamlet,* no doubt in tribute
to the writer who strongly influenced his own work and to the
play from which he often borrowed language and ideas.

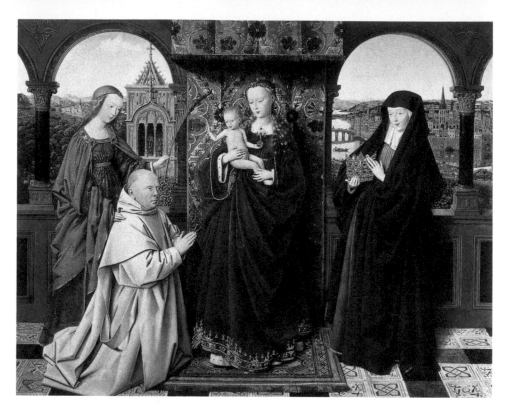

Jan van Eyck Active 1422–1441

Van Eyck, born probably at Maaseyck in the province of Limburg,
is first recorded in 1422 working at The Hague for the Count of Holland.
In 1425 he was named court painter to Philip the Good, Duke of
Burgundy, for whom he also undertook frequent diplomatic missions.
Most of his datable paintings were executed in Bruges in the 1430s.

Virgin and Child, with Saints and Donor

Oil, on panel, 18⅝ × 24⅛ in. (47.3 × 61.3 cm.). Painted probably
in the early 1440s. Acc. No. 54.1.161.

The Virgin and Child are flanked by St. Barbara, with her
attribute, the tower in which she was imprisoned, rising
behind her, and St. Elizabeth of Hungary, who gave up the
crown she carries to become a nun. The kneeling Carthusian
monk is Jan Vos, prior of the Charterhouse of Genadedal,
near Bruges, who commissioned the work. Many attempts
have been made to identify the walled town at right, but
despite the remarkably vivid details the view appears to
be imaginary. Most modern scholars consider this one of van
Eyck's last paintings, begun by him in 1441 but completed in
his shop, possibly with the aid of Petrus Christus (d. 1472/73).

Jean-Honoré Fragonard 1732–1806

Brought to Paris at an early age, Fragonard worked briefly with Chardin and then with Boucher. In 1752 he won the Prix de Rome, and in 1756 he began five years of study in Italy. After his return he was much in demand at the court of Louis XV for his blithe pastoral scenes, landscapes, and decorative paintings. Fragonard held various public offices during the Revolution but lost them all under the Directory. He died in poverty.

The Progress of Love

Oil, on canvas (for individual specifications see separate list). Acc. Nos. 15.1.45–15.1.55.

The first four panels of this series—*The Pursuit, The Meeting, The Lover Crowned,* and *Love Letters*—were commissioned by Madame du Barry for a new dining pavilion in the garden of her château at Louveciennes, overlooking the Seine west of Paris. Begun probably in 1771, they were seen at Louveciennes in 1772 and described in the press as not yet finished, but subsequently they were rejected, possibly because their style seemed old-fashioned in a building designed in the new classicizing manner. Joseph-Marie Vien provided replacements in the "antique" taste, and Fragonard retained his paintings until, in 1790, he retired for a year to his native Grasse. There he installed the four original panels in the main salon of his cousin Maubert's house and, to complete the decoration, painted two more large panels, four overdoors with Cupids, and four slender panels with hollyhocks. Though the full meaning of the individual panels and of the series as a whole has yet to be satisfactorily explained, the Frick canvases, with their grand scale and elaborate compositions, are not only major examples of Fragonard's art but rank among the outstanding achievements of French decorative painting of the eighteenth century.

The Progress of Love

The Pursuit (15.1.45)
125 ⅛ × 84 ⅞ in. (317.8 × 215.5 cm.).

The Meeting (15.1.46)
125 × 96 in. (317.5 × 243.8 cm.).

The Lover Crowned (15.1.48)
125 ⅛ × 95 ¾ in. (317.8 × 243.2 cm.).

Love Letters (15.1.47)
124 ⅞ × 85 ⅜ in. (317.1 × 216.8 cm.).

NOS. 45-48. Signed: *fragonard.*
Painted between 1771 and 1773.

Reverie (15.1.49)
125 ⅛ × 77 ⅝ in. (317.8 × 197.1 cm.).

Love Triumphant (15.1.50)
125 × 56 ½ in. (317.5 × 143.5 cm.).

Love the Avenger (15.1.51)
59 ⅜ × 50 ⅜ in. (150.8 × 127.9 cm.).

Love Pursuing a Dove (15.1.52)
59 ⅝ × 47 ¾ in. (151.4 × 121.2 cm.).

Love the Jester (15.1.53)
59 ⅜ × 50 ⅜ in. (150.8 × 127.9 cm.).

Love the Sentinel (15.1.54)
57 ⅝ × 47 ½ in. (146.3 × 120.6 cm.).

Hollyhocks (15.1.55 A-D)
Nos. 55 A, C, 125 ¼ × 25 in. (318.2 × 63.5 cm.); Nos. 55 B, D,
125 ½ × 16 ⅜ in. (318.8 × 41.6 cm.).

NOS. 49–55. Painted 1790–91.

The Pursuit

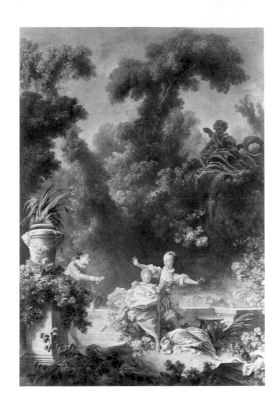

The Meeting

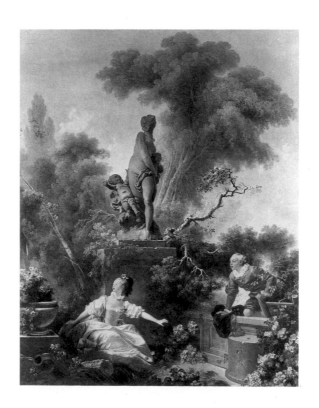

The Lover Crowned

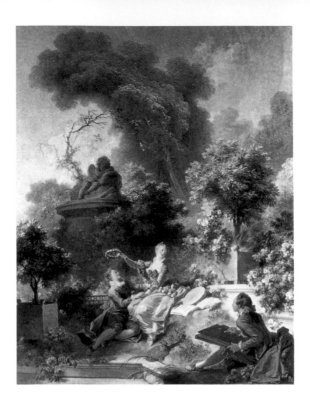

Love Letters

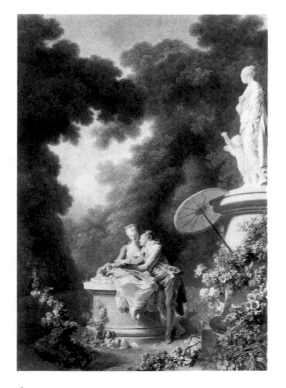

Reverie

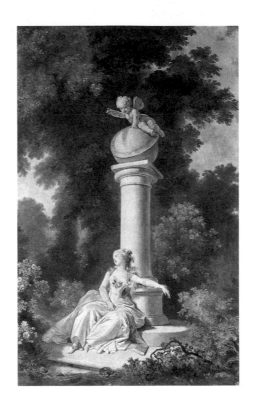

Love Triumphant

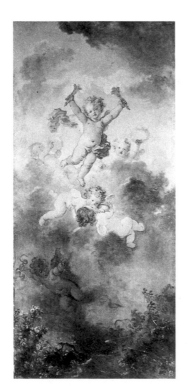

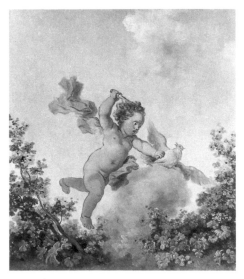

Love the Avenger

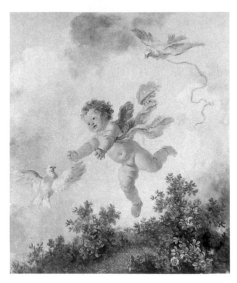

Love Pursuing a Dove

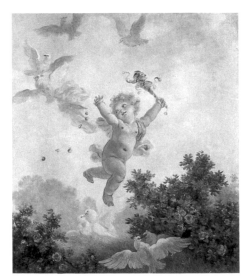

Love the Jester

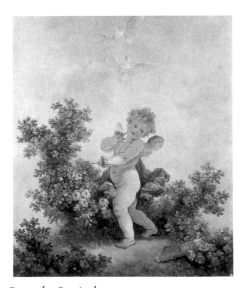

Love the Sentinel

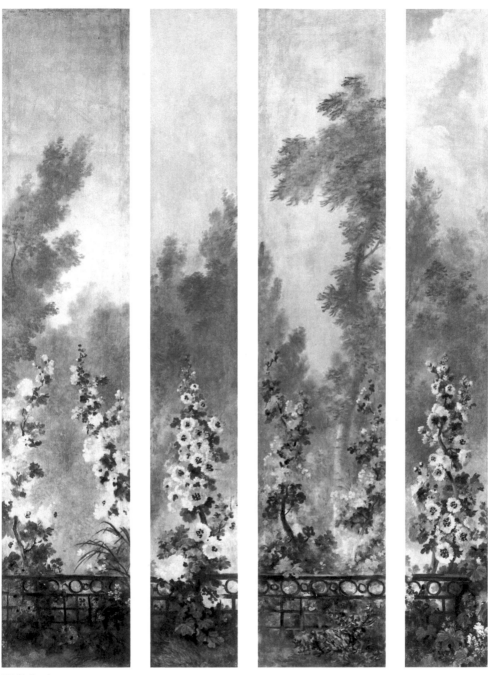

Hollyhocks

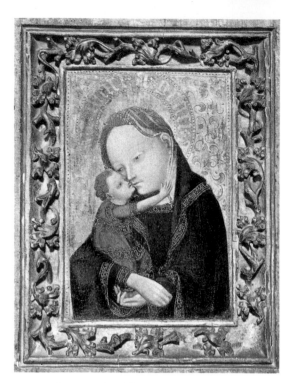

French, Probably Burgundian   About 1390–1400

Virgin and Child
Oil and tempera, on panel, 8⅝ × 5⅝ in. (21.9 × 14.3 cm.);
with frame, 12⅛ × 9¼ in. (30.8 × 23.5 cm.). Acc. No. 27.1.57.

The national origin of this panel is uncertain, as are the origins
of many late Gothic works. The artist appears to have been
familiar with contemporary Italian painting as well as with the
art of France and Flanders. The tender sentiment, rich coloring,
and decorative patterning are associated with many European
centers, but the style comes closest to Burgundian painting
of the late fourteenth century. The panel and its frame carved
with spiraling vines are made from a single piece of wood.

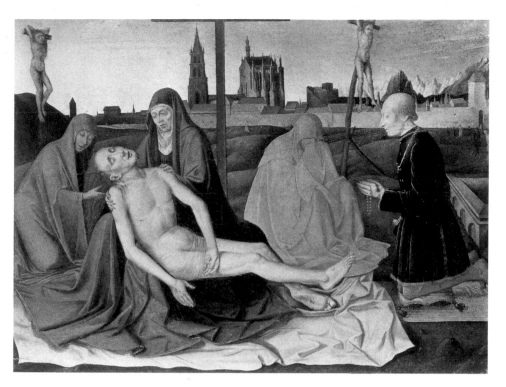

French, Probably South of France Fifteenth Century

Pietà with Donor
Tempera or mixed technique, on panel, 15⅝ × 22 in.
(39.7 × 55.8 cm.). Acc. No. 07.1.56.

The Pietà, a representation of the Virgin supporting the dead
Christ in a pose that poignantly recalls the image of her
holding the Child, is a motif that first appears in Germanic
art of the fourteenth century. Here the figures are set in a
landscape which includes Christ's sepulcher at right behind
the unidentified donor, a Gothic city representing Jerusalem,
and distant snowcapped mountains. This panel, once attributed
to Antonello da Messina, now is believed to have been painted
in Savoy or Provence during the middle or final third of the
fifteenth century. It is an enlarged copy with variations of a
Pietà without donor also in The Frick Collection (see Konrad
Witz, Follower of, p. 159).

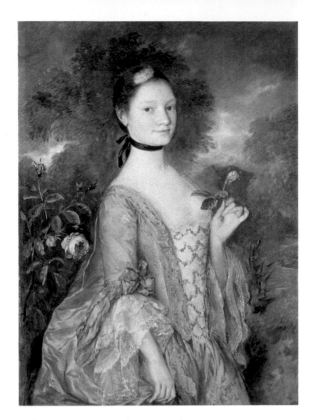

Thomas Gainsborough 1727–1788

Gainsborough left his native Suffolk in 1740 for London, where he worked with the French engraver Gravelot and probably with Francis Hayman. He moved to Ipswich about 1752 and to the fashionable resort of Bath in 1759, returning to London only in 1774. Best known for his portraits, he also painted numerous landscapes.

Sarah, Lady Innes
Oil, on canvas, 40 × 28⅝ in. (101.6 × 72.7 cm.).
Painted about 1757. Acc. No. 14.1.58.

According to family tradition the sitter was Sarah, daughter and heiress of Thomas Hodges of Ipswich. She married Sir William Innes, captain of the Second Light Dragoons, and died in 1770. This portrait, painted early in Gainsborough's career, is still somewhat stiff in its mannered pose, but the diaphanous fabrics and softly brushed landscape presage the artist's mature style.

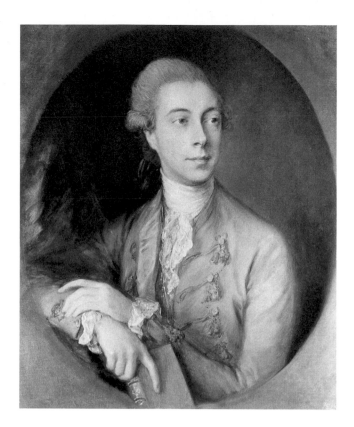

Gainsborough **Richard Paul Jodrell**
Oil, on canvas, 30¼ × 25⅛ in. (76.8 × 63.8 cm.).
Painted about 1774. Acc. No. 46.1.154.

Richard Jodrell (1745–1831) was an antiquarian, philologist, and dramatist, a Member of Parliament, and a friend of Dr. Johnson. To judge from his apparent age he must have posed for this portrait toward the end of Gainsborough's Bath period or shortly after the artist had moved to London. With its technique of transparent glazes of color the painting exhibits a quality that Gainsborough's great rival Sir Joshua Reynolds singled out for praise: "the lightness of effect which is so eminent a beauty in his work."

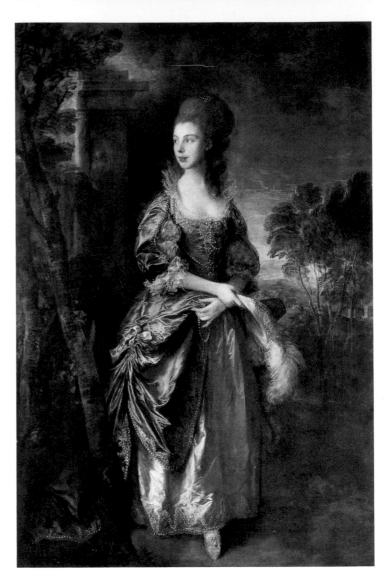

Gainsborough   **The Hon. Frances Duncombe**
Oil, on canvas, 92¼ × 61⅛ in. (234.3 × 155.2 cm.).
Painted about 1777. Acc. No. 11.1.61.

Frances (1757–1827), daughter of Anthony Duncombe, Baron
of Downton, Wiltshire, was married in 1778 to John
Bowater of London. Gainsborough also painted a half-length
portrait of her dated 1773. The Frick canvas testifies to the
artist's admiration for Van Dyck, not only in its elegant
proportions, graceful pose, and Arcadian setting, but even in the
costume, which recalls fashions of the seventeenth century.

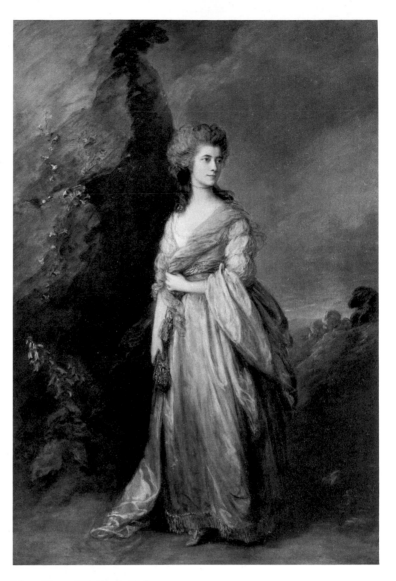

Gainsborough **Mrs. Peter William Baker**
Oil, on canvas, 89⅝ × 59¾ in. (227.6 × 151.8 cm.).
Signed and dated: *Thos. Gainsborough/1781*. Acc. No. 17.1.59.

Jane (d. 1816), daughter of James Clitherow of Boston House,
Middlesex, married Peter Baker of Ranston, Dorsetshire, in
1781—the year of this portrait. The windswept natural setting,
which recalls the landscape paintings of Gainsborough's
late years, invests this classically simple composition with a
feeling of movement and drama.

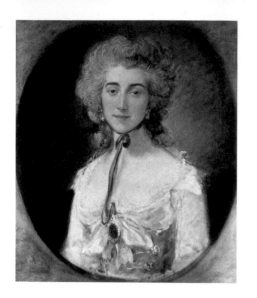 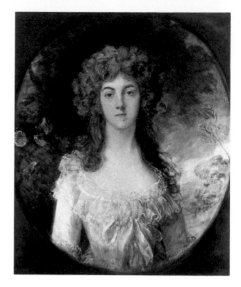

Gainsborough   **Grace Dalrymple Elliott**
Oil, on canvas, 30⅛ × 25 in. (76.5 × 63.5 cm.).
Painted probably in 1782. Acc. No. 46.1.153.

Grace Dalrymple (c. 1754–1823), daughter of an Edinburgh
barrister, married Sir John Elliott in 1771 but was divorced
by him five years later. A remarkably tall and striking woman,
she gained considerable notoriety through her liaisons with such
prominent figures as the Prince of Wales, who may have
commissioned this portrait, and Philippe Égalité, Duc
d'Orléans, whose mistress she was at the time of the French
Revolution. When the portrait was exhibited at the Royal
Academy in 1782 it evoked much comment; the hair was
criticized, and the subject's high coloring and expression were
said to denote her calling.

Mrs. Charles Hatchett
Oil, on canvas, 29¾ × 24⅝ in. (75.5 × 62.5 cm.).
Painted perhaps in 1786. Acc. No. 03.1.60.

Elizabeth Collick (c. 1766–1837), a gifted pianist and pupil
of Clementi, married Charles Hatchett of London, discoverer
of the metallic element columbium (now called niobium)
and friend of many of the leading intellectuals of his day. The
Hatchetts appear to have been on close terms with
Gainsborough, who shared their love of music.

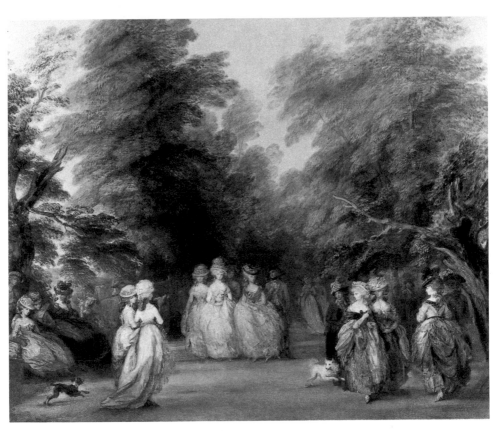

Gainsborough **The Mall in St. James's Park**
Oil, on canvas, 47½ × 57⅞ in. (120.6 × 147 cm.).
Painted probably in 1783. Acc. No. 16.1.62.

St. James's Park was near Gainsborough's London residence, Schomberg House, in Pall Mall. *The Mall,* with its carefully arranged figure groups combined in a landscape setting, is unusual among the artist's later works and recalls, as several contemporary critics remarked, the *fêtes galantes* of Watteau. The feathery foliage and rhythmic design led one observer to describe the painting as "all aflutter, like a lady's fan." Another reported that the artist composed the painting partly from dolls and a model of the setting. Attempts to identify the ladies in the central group as the daughters of George III and the background figure under the trees at right as the artist himself are attractive but unsubstantiated.

Gentile da Fabriano c. 1370–1427

Gentile was born in Fabriano, near Urbino, but is first recorded in 1408 in Venice. He worked there, in Brescia, and probably in other North Italian towns before moving around 1420 to Tuscany, where for the next few years he received important commissions from churches and great families of Siena, Florence, and Orvieto. By 1427 he had left for Rome to paint a series of frescoes, now lost, in St. John Lateran.

Madonna and Child, with Saints Lawrence and Julian

Tempera, on panel, 35¾ × 18½ in. (90.8 × 47 cm.).
Signed, on the frame: *gentili[s?] [de?]* .... Painted about 1423–25.
Acc. No. 66.1.167.

This small but richly painted altarpiece was designed perhaps for some private family chapel. It must be close in date to Gentile's best-known work, the *Adoration of the Magi* of 1423, commissioned by the Strozzi family of Florence and now in the Uffizi. Like the *Adoration,* this panel, with its elegantly ornamented surface of glittering gold leaf and brilliant color, perpetuates late Gothic traditions, most obviously in the gentle, graceful figures of the Madonna and Child. The adoring saints, however, seem more advanced than work of the same date by Gentile's Florentine contemporaries; the portrait-like heads and solidly modeled bodies are strikingly natural and eloquent. St. Lawrence, the third-century Roman deacon, kneels at left beside the grid on which he was burned alive. At right, wearing knightly robes and sword, is St. Julian the Hospitaler, who built a refuge for travelers.

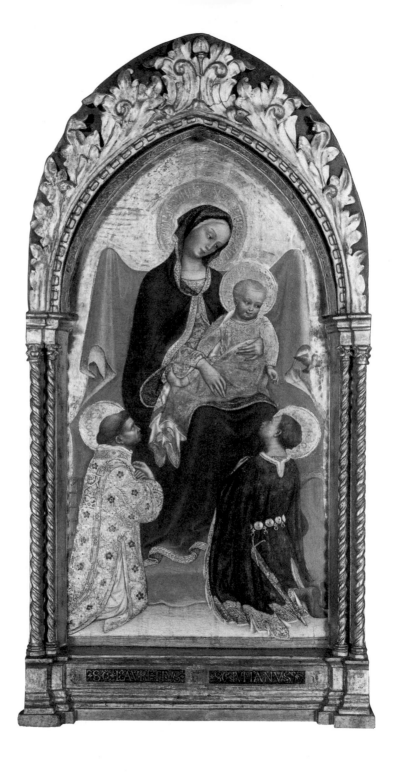

73

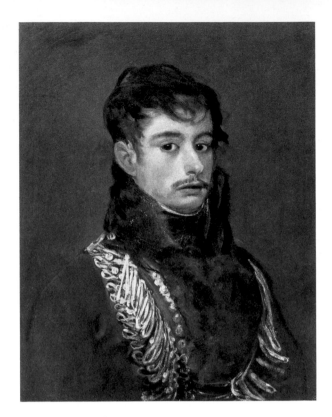

Francisco de Goya y Lucientes 1746–1828

Born in Fuendetodos, Goya served his apprenticeship in nearby Saragossa and then studied with Francisco Bayeu in Madrid. He was in Italy in 1771, worked in Saragossa the following year, and in 1774 became a designer for the Royal Tapestry Factory. Appointed court painter to Charles III in 1786, he continued in that post under Charles IV and Ferdinand VII. In addition to portraits Goya painted historical, religious, and genre subjects, bitter satires, and demonological fantasies; he also was a brilliant graphic artist. In 1824, out of favor with the court, he left Spain and settled in Bordeaux, where he died.

An Officer (Conde de Tepa?)

Oil, on canvas, 24⅞ × 19¼ in. (63.2 × 48.9 cm.).
Acc. No. 14.1.64.

The intense and wary young officer who posed for this portrait has yet to be convincingly identified, though several candidates have been put forward. The most likely is Don Francisco Leandro de Viana, Conde de Tepa, who was active in colonial affairs and whose wife had vast holdings in Mexico.

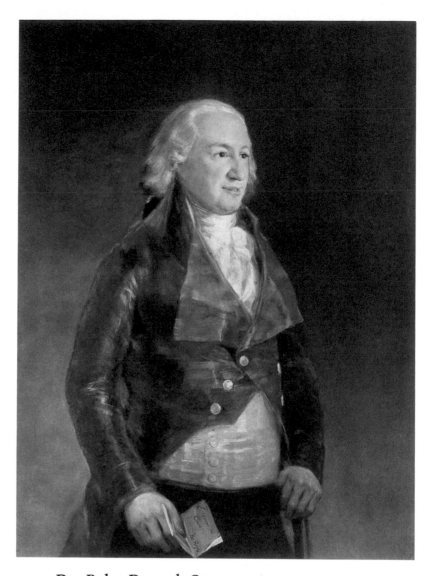

Goya

Don Pedro, Duque de Osuna
Oil, on canvas, 44½ × 32¾ in. (113 × 83.2 cm.).
Signed: *Por Goya*. Painted probably in the 1790s. Acc.
No. 43.1.151.

Don Pedro de Alcántara Téllez-Girón y Pacheco (1755–1807),
ninth Duque de Osuna, was one of Spain's wealthiest and most
talented noblemen during the reigns of Charles III and
Charles IV. After the Royal court he and his wife were Goya's
most faithful patrons, commissioning more than twenty-four
works including portraits, religious subjects, and a famous set
of decorative canvases for their country palace outside Madrid.

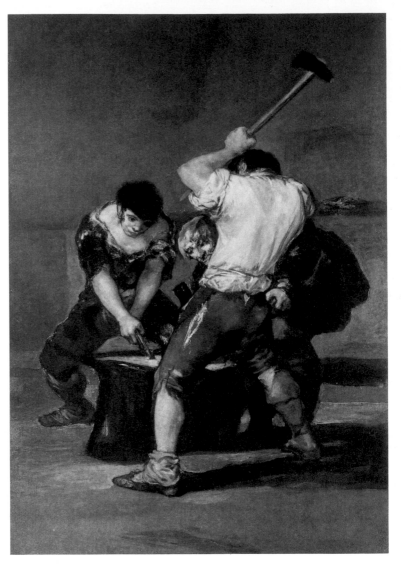

Goya

The Forge
Oil, on canvas, 71½ × 49¼ in. (181.6 × 125.1 cm.).
Painted about 1815–20. Acc. No. 14.1.65.

The composition of this canvas derives from traditional
depictions of the forge of Vulcan, the metalworker of the
Olympian gods. Goya, however, translates the theme into
contemporary language, using sturdy laborers in working
clothes as a subject suitable for monumental treatment. The
rough, vigorous application of paint and somber coloring
heighten the power and intensity of the figures and their
actions.

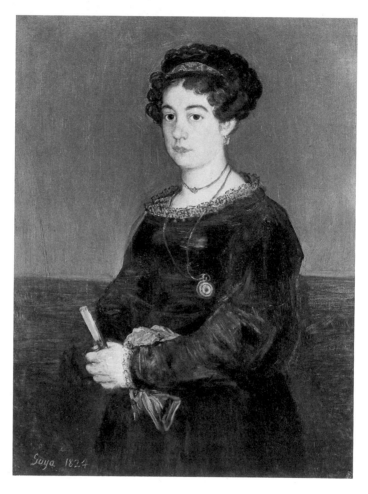

Goya

Doña María Martínez de Puga
Oil, on canvas, 31½ × 23 in. (80 × 58.4 cm.).
Signed and dated: *Goya 1824*. Acc. No. 14.1.63.

The almost monochromatic palette and broad brushwork
employed here are characteristic of Goya's last portraits. The
date of the canvas indicates that it could have been painted in
Madrid shortly before the artist left Spain or in Paris or
Bordeaux later that year. Of the various identities that have
been proposed for the sitter none has been verified, and even
her presumed name, supplied by a previous owner, is in question.

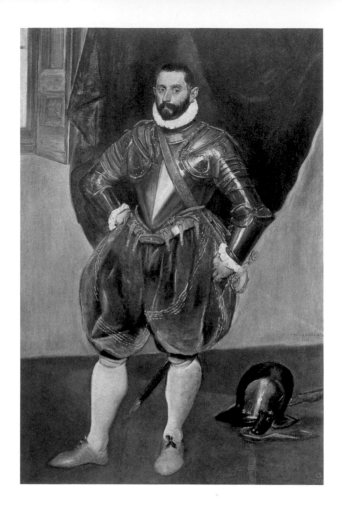

El Greco 1541–1614

Domenikos Theotokopoulos, called El Greco, was born in the
Venetian dependency of Crete. As a youth he traveled to Venice,
where he reputedly studied with Titian. He was in Rome in 1570
and by 1577 had settled in Toledo, where he spent his remaining
years. His work consists chiefly of religious subjects and portraits.

Vincenzo Anastagi

Oil, on canvas, 74 × 49⅞ in. (188 × 126.7 cm.). Signed in
Greek characters. Painted about 1571–76. Acc. No. 13.1.68.

Vincenzo Anastagi (c. 1531–86) joined the Knights of Malta in
1563 and was a leader in the heroic defense of that island during
the massive Turkish siege of 1565. He later became sergeant
major of Castel Sant'Angelo in Rome. This portrait, Venetian
in conception but already characteristically intense and spirited
in style, probably dates from El Greco's last years in Italy.

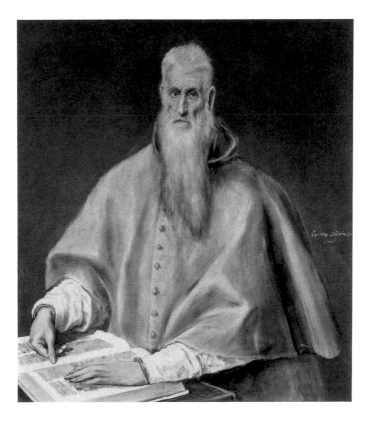

El Greco

St. Jerome

Oil, on canvas, 43½ × 37½ in. (110.5 × 95.3 cm.).
Signed in Greek characters. Painted about 1590–1600.
Acc. No. 05.1.67.

St. Jerome (c. 342–420), one of the four great Doctors of the
Western Church, is venerated for his ascetic piety and for his
monumental Latin translation of the Bible, represented here
by the large volume on which he rests his hands. Following
an old convention the artist depicts him in the robes of a cardinal.
This composition proved popular and was produced in at
least four versions by El Greco and his shop.

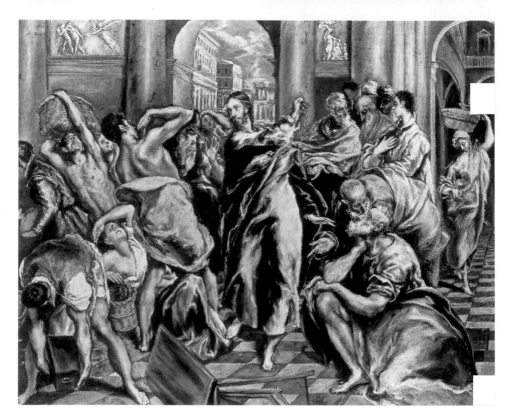

El Greco **Purification of the Temple**
Oil, on canvas, 16½ × 20⅝ in. (41.9 × 52.4 cm.).
Painted about 1600. Acc. No.09.1.66.

The subject of Christ driving the traders and moneychangers
from the Temple assumed special significance during the
Counter Reformation as a symbolic reference to the
purification of the Church. The theme absorbed El Greco
throughout his career, as is demonstrated by the many versions
of this composition that issued from his shop. The Frick
canvas, one of the later examples, is small in size but generates
remarkable dramatic intensity through its explosive movement
and cold but brilliant coloring.

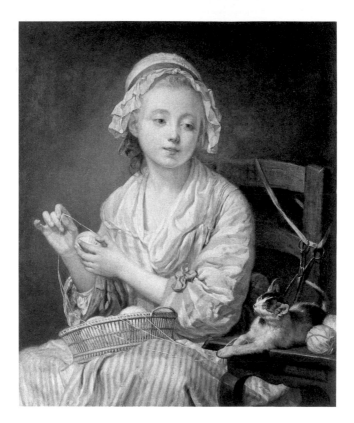

Jean-Baptiste Greuze 1725–1805

*Greuze left his native Burgundy for Paris about 1750 and studied
at the Academy. He first exhibited at the Salon in 1755, and later
that year he began a long sojourn in Italy. He was made a full
Academy member in 1769. Greuze's anecdotal, often moralizing
genre scenes and his incisive portraits won him great popular
acclaim and the enthusiastic support of Diderot.*

The Wool Winder

Oil, on canvas, 29⅜ × 24⅛ in. (74.6 × 61.3 cm.).
Painted probably in 1759. Acc. No. 43.1.148.

Like much of Greuze's early work *The Wool Winder* is related
to Chardin's genre pictures of the 1730s, but Greuze's scenes
are usually, as here, more whimsical and anecdotal. The letter B
carved into the top rail of the chair suggests that the subject
may have been a younger sister of the artist's wife, Anne-
Gabrielle Babuti.

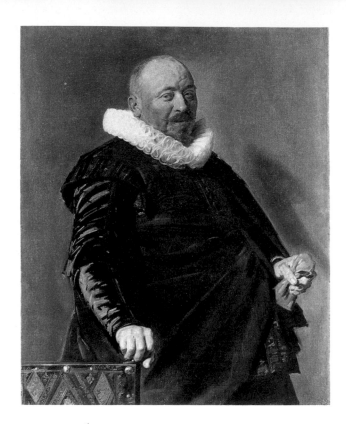

Frans Hals 1581/85–1666

*Hals probably was born in Antwerp, but by 1591 his family had
moved to Haarlem, where he is believed to have studied with Carel van
Mander. He joined the painters' guild of Haarlem in 1610 and worked
in that city until his death, painting chiefly portraits, including several
large group portraits of militia companies and the regents of
charitable institutions.*

Portrait of an Elderly Man
Oil, on canvas, 45½ × 36 in. (115.6 × 91.4 cm.).
Painted about 1627–30. Acc. No. 10.1.69.

The technique of this portrait dating from Hals' early maturity
is derived in part from Rubens. The thin, fluid handling of
paint, the warm but restricted color scheme, and the subject's
animated expression and self-confident air are typical of
Hals' major works from those years.

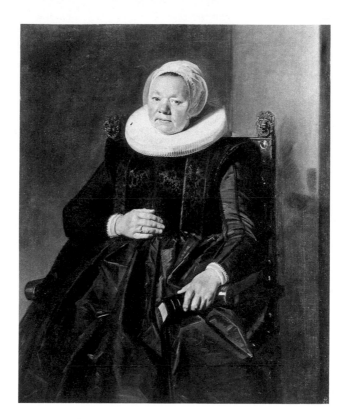

Hals

Portrait of a Woman
Oil, on canvas, 45⅞ × 36¾ in. (116.5 × 93.3 cm.).
Dated: *1635*. Acc. No. 10.1.72.

An inscription at upper left gives the age of the unidentified
sitter as fifty-six. The portrait records her features with
objectivity and with a blunt, vigorous brushwork that seems
in itself to reflect her character. Like most of Hals' works,
this one employs a plain background well suited to his
unpretentious style of portraiture.

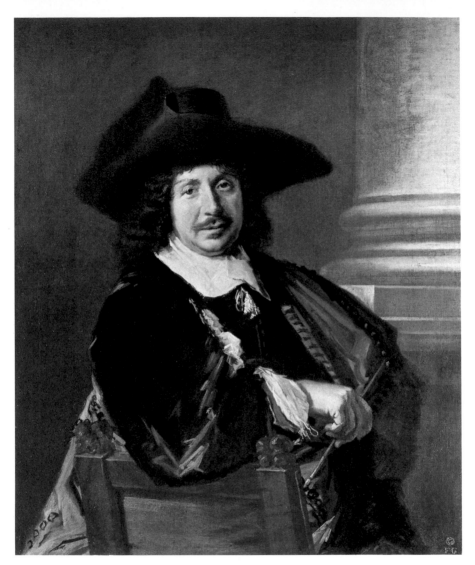

Hals

Portrait of a Painter
Oil, on canvas, 39½ × 32⅝ in. (100.3 × 82.9 cm.).
Painted probably in the early 1650s. Spurious signature and
date: F.H. / 16[5?]—. Acc. No.06.1.71.

This canvas was once considered a self-portrait, but comparison
with known likenesses of Hals makes the identification
improbable. The painting was altered at some time by the
addition of the column at right and by areas of retouching
in the hand and parts of the costume. Nevertheless, the strongly
modeled head, with its alert, quizzical aspect, is characteristic
of Hals' portraiture at its best.

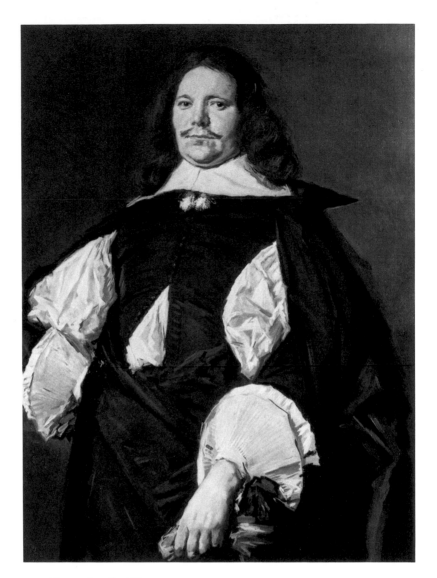

Hals

Portrait of a Man
Oil, on canvas, 44½ × 32¼ in. (113 × 81.9 cm.).
Signed: FH. Painted probably about 1660. Acc. No. 17.1.70.

Once erroneously believed to represent the seventeenth-century
Dutch naval hero Michiel de Ruyter, this portrait of an unknown
man appears to have been painted when Hals was already
well over seventy. By then he had developed the flashing
bravura technique—particularly evident in the drapery and
gloves—that would later influence Manet.

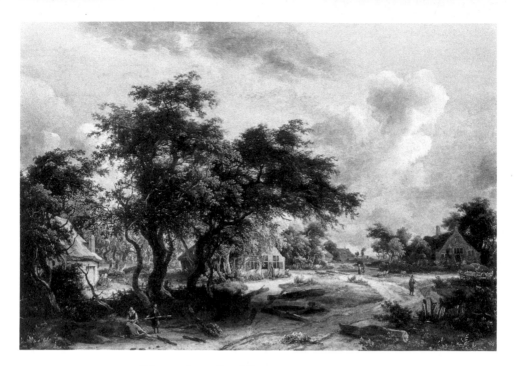

Meyndert Hobbema 1638–1709

In 1657 Hobbema was apprenticed in his native Amsterdam to Jacob van Ruisdael, whose style and subject matter had a profound influence on him. Hobbema painted landscapes prolifically until 1668, when he was appointed municipal assessor of wine-measures. Relatively few works appear to date from his last forty years.

Village Among Trees

Oil, on oak panel, 30 × 43 ½ in. (76.2 × 110.5 cm.).
Signed and dated: *m. hobbema | f. 1665*. Acc. No. 02.1.73.

This panel, painted during Hobbema's most active period, is composed of elements he employed repeatedly throughout his career: large trees with variegated foliage, picturesque cottages, a low sky with wind-swept clouds, and a rutted road that winds into the far distance.

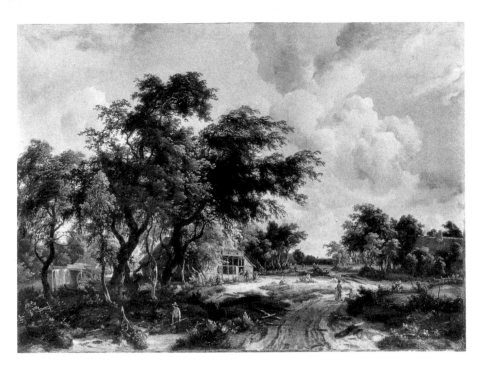

Hobbema

Village with Water Mill Among Trees
Oil, on canvas, 37⅛ × 51⅛ in. (94.3 × 129.8 cm.).
Signed: *meynd ʳᵗ hobbema*. Acc. No. 11.1.74.

Comparison of this canvas with the preceding *Village Among Trees,* which dates from about the same time, clearly demonstrates that if Hobbema's repertory of motifs observed in nature was limited, he nevertheless invested his paintings with considerable freshness and variety. No other major Dutch landscapist was so economical of design and visual material.

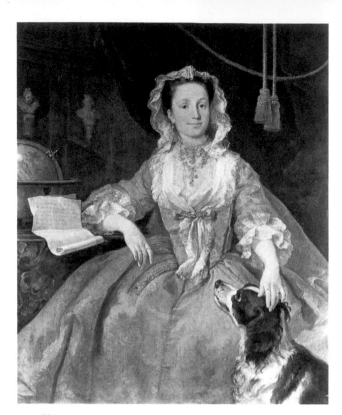

William Hogarth 1697-1764

A life-long resident of London, Hogarth was apprenticed to an engraver of silver plate at fifteen and later studied drawing with Thornhill. His fame among his contemporaries derived chiefly from the series of moral satires, such as The Rake's Progress *and* Marriage à la Mode, *that he engraved after his own oil paintings. He also produced portraits and was the author of an autobiography and a treatise on aesthetics.*

Miss Mary Edwards

Oil, on canvas, 49¾ × 37⅞ in. (126.4 × 101.3 cm.).
Signed and dated: W. HOGARTH 1742. Acc. No. 14.1.75.

Mary Edwards (1705–43), one of the richest women of her time, was married clandestinely to Lord Anne Hamilton, a younger son of the fourth Duke of Hamilton. A few years later, in order to protect her fortune from her extravagant husband, she repudiated the marriage, though it was tantamount to declaring her infant son illegitimate. Hogarth's straight-forward, lively style of portraiture clearly suited the strong personality of his subject.

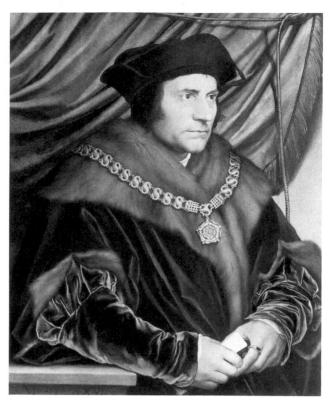

Hans Holbein the Younger 1497/98–1543

Holbein was the son of the Augsburg painter Hans Holbein the Elder, who probably gave him his first training. By 1515 he was working in Basel, where he achieved great success. He lived in England from 1526 to 1528 and four years later returned to settle there, eventually becoming court painter to Henry VIII.

Sir Thomas More

Oil, on oak panel, 29½ × 23¾ in. (74.9 × 60.3 cm.).
Dated: M.D.XXVII. Acc. No. 12.1.77.

Thomas More (1477/78–1535), humanist scholar, author, and statesman, served Henry VIII as diplomatic envoy and Privy Councillor prior to his election as speaker of the House of Commons in 1523. In 1529 he succeeded Cardinal Wolsey as Lord Chancellor, but three years later he resigned that office over the issue of Henry's divorce, and subsequently he refused to subscribe to the Act of Supremacy. For this he was convicted of high treason and beheaded. He was canonized in 1935. Holbein's incisive characterization of More and his brilliant rendering of the rich costume make this one of his best and most popular paintings.

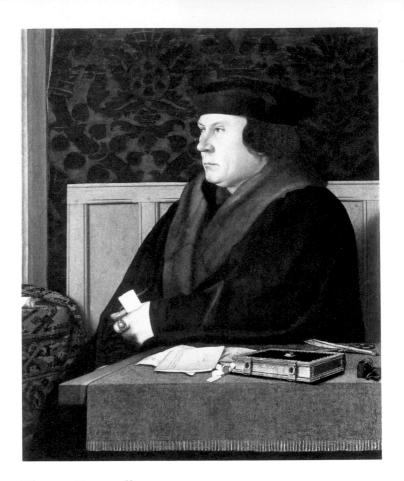

Holbein

Thomas Cromwell
Oil, on oak panel, 30⅞ × 25⅜ in. (78.4 × 64.4 cm.).
Acc. No. 15.1.76.

Thomas Cromwell (c. 1485–1540) was the son of a London
blacksmith and tavern-keeper. He entered Cardinal Wolsey's
service in 1514 and held various high offices under Henry VIII,
culminating in his appointment as Lord Great Chamberlain
in 1539. He was largely responsible for the execution of Thomas
More. In 1540 Cromwell fell from Henry's favor and was
himself accused of treason and beheaded. Of the several
versions of this portrait the Frick example is considered the
best and oldest, but all probably derive from a lost original.

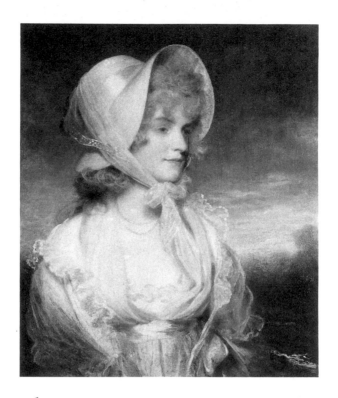

John Hoppner 1758–1810

Hoppner spent his boyhood as a chorister at St. James's Palace before entering the Royal Academy in 1775. He first exhibited at the Academy in 1780, and in 1795 he became full Academician. He enjoyed great popularity as a portraitist, serving in that capacity to the Prince of Wales (later George IV).

The Hon. Lucy Byng
Oil, on canvas, 30⅛ × 25 in. (76.5 × 63.5 cm.).
Acc. No. 99.1.79.

Some uncertainty exists over the identity of the subject, who may have been either Lucy Elizabeth Byng (1794–1875), daughter of Vice-Admiral George Byng, sixth Viscount Torrington, or another Lucy Elizabeth Byng, daughter of George Byng, fourth Viscount Torrington. Hoppner's feathery brushwork did not vary sufficiently over the years to permit a dating on stylistic grounds.

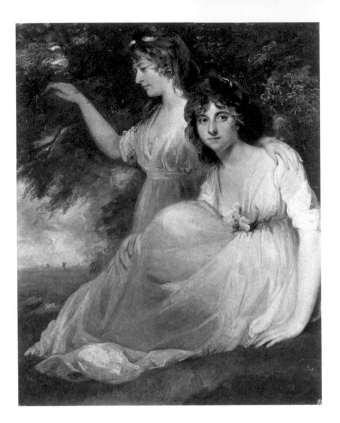

Hoppner

The Ladies Sarah and Catherine Bligh
Oil, on canvas, 51⅛ × 40⅜ in. (129.8 × 102.5 cm.).
Painted about 1790. Acc. No. 15.1.80.

Lady Sarah Bligh (1772–97), kneeling, and her sister Lady
Catherine (1774–1812) were the youngest children of John
Bligh, third Earl of Darnley. The open water with distant sails in
the background of this portrait may represent the Thames at
Gravesend as seen from the Bligh estate of Cobham Park.

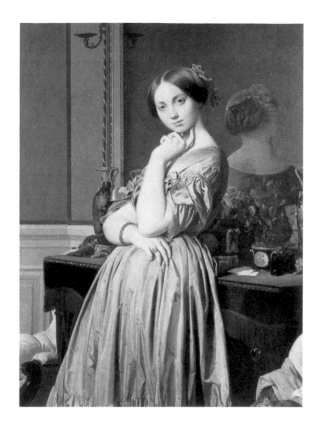

Jean-Auguste-Dominique Ingres 1780–1867

Born in Montauban, Ingres studied first in nearby Toulouse and then with David in Paris. He won the Prix de Rome in 1801 and was in Italy from 1806 until 1824. He spent the following decade in Paris, where he received official honors and attracted many pupils, then returned to Rome for seven years as Director of the French Academy. His final years were spent in Paris.

Comtesse d'Haussonville

Oil, on canvas, 51⅞ × 36¼ in. (131.8 × 92 cm.).
Signed and dated: INGRES./1845. Acc. No. 27.1.81.

Louise, Princesse de Broglie (1818–82), married at the age of eighteen. Her husband was a diplomat, writer, and member of the French Academy, and she herself published a number of books, including a life of Byron. This portrait, begun in 1842, was the fruit of several false starts and a great many preparatory drawings, one of which is in The Frick Collection. According to a letter written by the artist, the finished work "aroused a storm of approval."

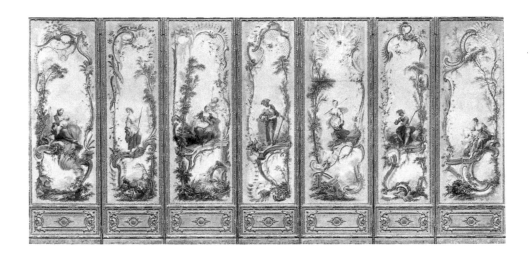

Jacques de Lajoue, Attributed to 1686/87–1761

The son of an architect, Lajoue was born in Paris. By 1721 he was
an associate of the Academy, where he exhibited until 1753. A painter
of landscapes, seascapes, interiors, and animal studies, he assisted
in the decoration of many châteaux and palaces.

Seven Decorative Panels Mounted in a Screen
Oil, on canvas: Nos. 82A, C, E, G, 58⅝ × 21½ in.
(148.9 × 54.6 cm.); Nos. 82B, D, F, 58⅝ × 17⅞ in.
(148.9 × 45.4 cm.). Painted perhaps in the 1730s.
Acc. Nos. 16.1.82 A–G.

At present mounted as a screen, these panels probably were
commissioned to be set in the walls of a room and may
originally have formed part of a larger suite representing
the twelve months. They are attributed to Lajoue on the basis
of their resemblance to his engraved designs and decorative
paintings, which employ similarly asymmetric compositions
and a profusion of shells, canopies, trellises, and consoles.

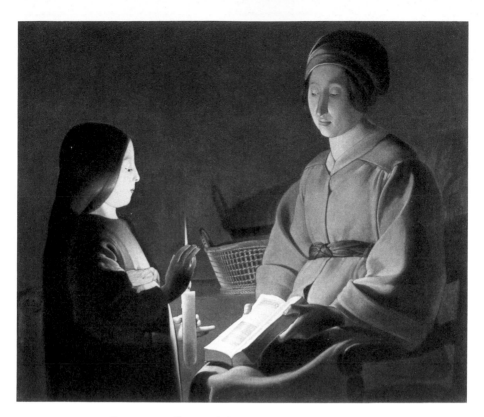

Georges de La Tour 1593–1652

Most of La Tour's life was spent in his native Lorraine, but his style, which appears to have been influenced by Caravaggio or his Dutch followers, suggests that he may have traveled abroad. A document of 1639 refers to him as "Peintre ordinaire du Roy," and he also worked for Lorraine's ducal court. He and his family died in an epidemic at Lunéville.

The Education of the Virgin
Oil, on canvas, 33 × 39½ in. (83.8 × 100.4 cm.).
Signed: *de la Tour f.* Painted about 1650. Acc. No. 48.1.155.

La Tour's striking use of light transfigures simple genre motifs and lends his scenes an air of mysterious significance. The subject of the education of the Virgin, who reads from a Bible held by her mother, St. Anne, first appears in fifteenth-century illuminated Books of Hours. Paintings closely similar to this one exist in several collections, and all may be workshop replicas of a lost original by La Tour.

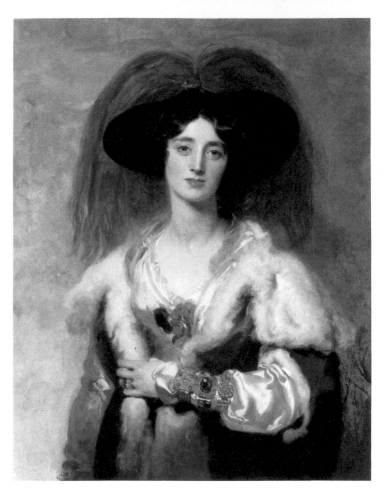

Sir Thomas Lawrence 1769–1830

Lawrence, born in Bristol, was appointed Painter to the King when only twenty-two. He entered the Royal Academy two years later, and in 1820 became its president. His portraits earned him a reputation on the Continent unequaled by any earlier British painter.

Julia, Lady Peel

Oil, on canvas, 35¾ × 27⅞ in. (90.8 × 70.8 cm.).
Painted in 1827. Acc. No.04.1.83.

Julia Floyd (1795–1859) was married in 1820 to the British statesman Sir Robert Peel, who twice served as Prime Minister and
was an avid patron of Lawrence. The Frick portrait apparently
was inspired by Rubens' painting of Susanne Fourment known
as the *Chapeau de paille,* which Peel had acquired in 1823. When
Lawrence's *Lady Peel* was first exhibited in 1827, a critic claimed
it to be among "the highest achievements of modern art."

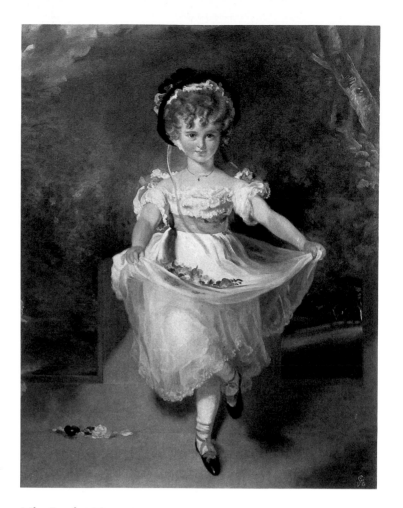

Lawrence

Miss Louisa Murray
Oil, on canvas, 36½ × 28⅞ in. (92.7 × 73.3 cm.).
Painted probably after 1827. Acc. No. 16.1.84.

Louisa Georgina Murray (1822–91) was the natural daughter
of Gen. the Rt. Hon. Sir George Murray, a soldier and
administrator. Of the several versions of Lawrence's portrait
of her, that in the Iveagh Bequest at Kenwood, London, is
considered the original. The Frick canvas probably is a
studio copy.

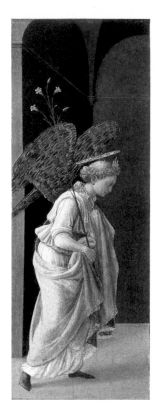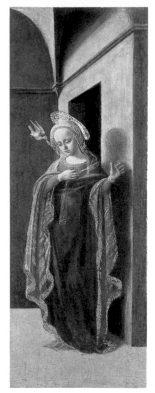

Fra Filippo Lippi c. 1406–1469

Florentine by birth, Fra Filippo took the vows of a Carmelite monk at about fifteen. He was in Padua in 1434, but in 1437 he returned to Florence, where he was employed by the Medici and other prominent families. He spent his last two years executing frescoes in the Cathedral at Spoleto.

The Annunciation

Tempera, on poplar panels: left panel, 25⅛ × 9⅞ in. (63.8 × 25.1 cm.); right panel, 25⅛ × 10 in. (63.8 × 25.4 cm.). Painted about 1440. Acc. No. 24.1.85.

The subject of the Annunciation was exceedingly popular in Florentine art of the mid-fifteenth century, and Fra Filippo depicted it often. The lily carried by the angel Gabriel in such scenes symbolizes the Virgin's purity, while the dove indicates the angel's words to her, "The Holy Ghost shall come upon thee." The two Frick panels, now framed together, probably originally formed the wings of a small altarpiece of which the central panel has been lost.

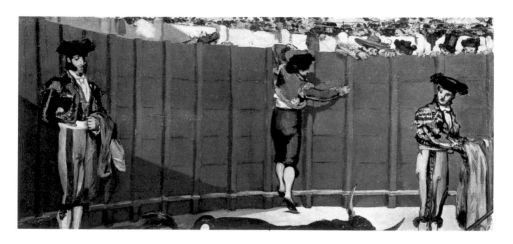

Édouard Manet 1832–1883

*Born into a prosperous Parisian household, Manet studied with
Couture. He first exhibited at the Salon in 1861, but two years later
he showed at the Salon des Refusés, where his work was received
with the ridicule that it provoked throughout most of his career. Official
recognition came to him only in the year before his death, when he
was awarded the Legion of Honor.*

The Bullfight

Oil, on canvas, 18⅞ × 42⅞ in. (47.9 × 108.9 cm.).
Signed: M. Painted in 1864. Acc. No. 14.1.86.

The Bullfight originally formed the upper part of a painting
Manet exhibited in the Salon of 1864 under the title *An Incident
in the Bullring.* After the Salon, possibly because the picture
was so scathingly reviewed and caricatured, the artist cut out
two separate compositions from the canvas, discarding a
narrow middle strip and a piece at upper left. The lower,
larger section, now known as *The Dead Toreador,* is in the
National Gallery, Washington. Such scenes attest to Manet's
enthusiasm both for Spain and for the art of Velázquez and Goya.

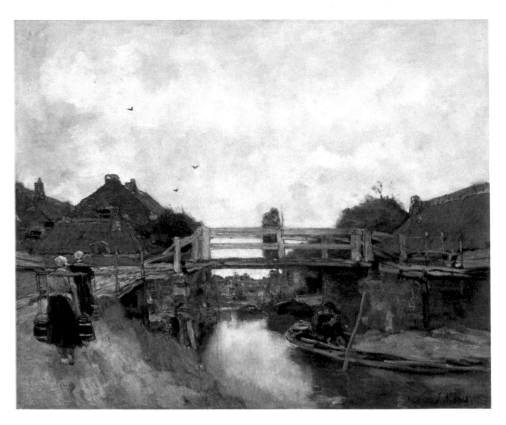

Jacobus Hendrikus Maris 1837–1899

Maris, born and trained in The Hague, spent the late 1860s in Paris, where he was influenced by the Barbizon landscapists. After his return to Holland in 1871 he became a leading figure in The Hague school of painting, together with his brothers Matthijs and Willem.

The Bridge

Oil, on canvas, 44⅜ × 54⅜ in. (112.7 × 138.1 cm.). Signed: *J. Maris*. Painted in 1885. Acc. No. 14.1.87.

The site depicted, said to be near Rijswijk on the outskirts of The Hague, was the subject of several related works by Maris, some of them perhaps preparatory studies for this painting. An impression of Maris' own etching of *The Bridge*, with the detail simplified and the composition reversed, also is in The Frick Collection.

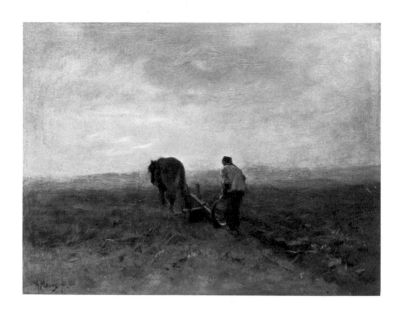

Anton Mauve 1838–1888

*Mauve studied in his native Zaandam, but the formative influence on
his style was that of the Maris brothers. After establishing a reputation
in Amsterdam he joined the group of prominent Dutch artists working
at The Hague. He won many prizes at international exhibitions
and was highly esteemed in both Europe and America.*

Early Morning Ploughing

Oil, on canvas, 16¾ × 22½ in. (42.5 × 57.2 cm.).
Signed: *A. Mauve p.* Acc. No. 77.1.170.

The artists of The Hague school resembled the Barbizon
painters in their reaction against academic art and in their
belief that nature and the common man provided the ideal
subject matter. But their landscapes usually are distinguished
from the more warmly colored works of their French contemporaries by a pervasive silvery gray atmosphere, so
characteristic of the Dutch climate. Mauve's young cousin
van Gogh, who studied with him, was much influenced in
his early period by such muted scenes of peasant life as
Early Morning Ploughing.

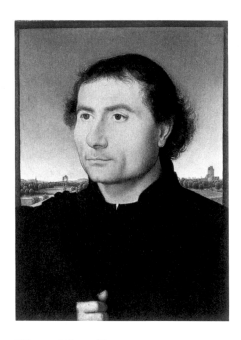

Hans Memling c. 1440–1494

*Born at Seligenstadt, near Frankfurt, Memling spent much of his life
in Bruges, where he was recorded as a new citizen in 1465. Two years
later he entered the Bruges painters' guild, and documents show that
he became one of the city's more prosperous residents. In addition
to portraits Memling painted many religious subjects.*

Portrait of a Man
Oil, on oak panel, 13⅛ × 9⅛ in. (33.5 × 23.2 cm.).
Acc. No. 68.1.169.

Though panels such as this often served as covers or wings
for small private altarpieces, it seems probable that the Frick
example, like many others dating from the second half of the
fifteenth century, was commissioned as an independent painting.
Memling was one of the most admired portraitists of his day,
in Italy as well as in northern Europe. His popularity was due
not only to his great skill in capturing physical likenesses,
but also to his even rarer gift for conveying the intellectual
and spiritual character of his subjects.

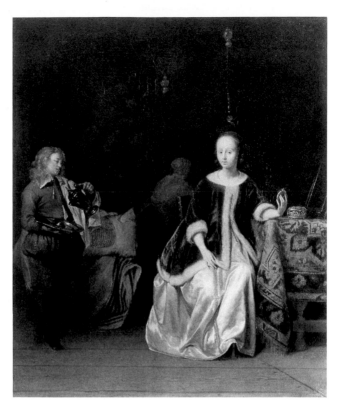

Gabriel Metsu 1629–1667

Metsu was born in Leyden and lived there at least until 1654, but by 1657 he had settled in Amsterdam. He painted genre scenes, small portraits, and religious subjects, and appears to have been influenced by Flemish painters and by his Dutch contemporaries ter Borch, de Hoogh, and Vermeer.

A Lady at Her Toilet

Oil, on canvas, 20⅜ × 16⅝ in. (51.7 × 42.2 cm.).
Signed: *G Metsu*. Painted about 1660. Acc. No.05.1.88.

In Amsterdam, Metsu produced a number of interior scenes inspired by ter Borch in their modest scale, finely painted detail, and richness of handling. As other artists were working in a closely similar vein, the attribution of this canvas is sometimes questioned, despite the apparent signature. Metsu's paintings, only modestly successful during his lifetime, were highly prized by eighteenth-century collectors.

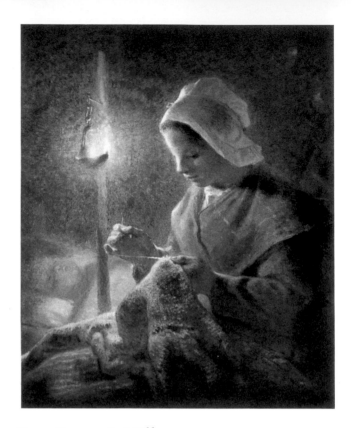

Jean-François Millet 1814–1875

The son of Norman peasants, Millet studied in Cherbourg and then Paris. His work was shown in several Salons in the 1840s, but it was not until the Winnower *of 1848 that he began to exhibit the peasant subjects that made him famous. In 1849 he moved to Barbizon, where he spent most of his remaining years.*

Woman Sewing by Lamplight

Oil, on canvas, 39⅝ × 32¼ in. (100.7 × 81.9 cm.).
Signed: *J. F. Millet.* Painted 1870–72. Acc. No. 06.1.89.

It has been suggested that Millet's many scenes of peasant women and their families working by lamplight were inspired by his fondness for Latin bucolic poetry, especially certain lines from Virgil's *Georgics.* Similar treatments by Rembrandt and other Dutch painters must also have influenced his choice of themes. The Frick canvas, finished in Barbizon in 1872, was begun two years earlier in Cherbourg, where Millet had moved his family to escape the invading Prussian armies.

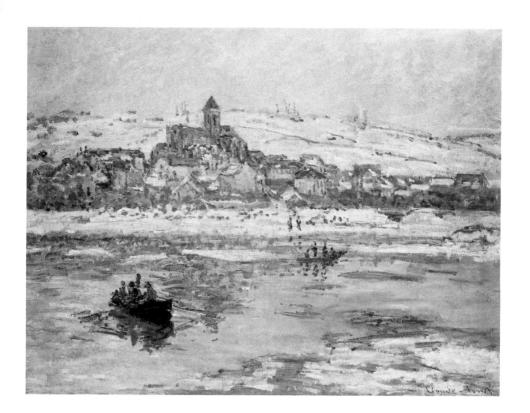

Claude-Oscar Monet 1840–1926

Parisian by birth, Monet spent his youth in Le Havre, where he worked with the painter Boudin. He returned to Paris in 1859 and showed in the Salons of 1865 and 1866. With Bazille, he organized the first Impressionist exhibition in 1874, which included works by Renoir, Pissarro, Boudin, Cézanne, and Degas. Monet painted in many parts of France as well as in Italy, Holland, and England. During his last years he worked chiefly in his gardens at Giverny.

Vétheuil in Winter

Oil, on canvas, 27 × 35⅜ in. (68.6 × 89.9 cm.).
Signed: *Claude Monet*. Painted in 1879. Acc. No. 42.1.146.

In 1878 Monet moved down the Seine from Argenteuil to Vétheuil, a small town which he painted from many different vantage points and in all seasons. The Frick canvas, executed almost entirely in blues and blue-greens with touches of rose tinting the snow and houses, vividly conveys an impression of the intense cold that occurred during the winter of 1879–80.

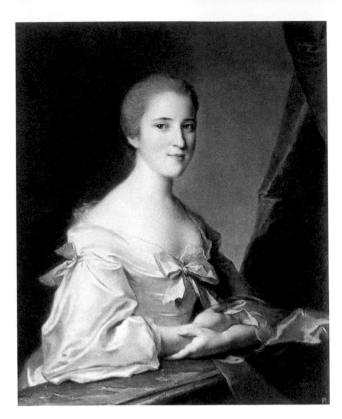

Jean-Marc Nattier 1685-1766

*Nattier, a Parisian, studied at the Academy and was already a
portraitist of note by the age of eighteen. In 1717 Peter the Great
summoned him to Holland to paint members of the visiting Russian
court, and the following year he became a member of the Academy.
He exhibited frequently in the Salons and received many commissions
from the court of Louis XV.*

Elizabeth, Countess of Warwick

Oil, on canvas, 32⅛ × 25¾ in. (81.5 × 65.4 cm.).
Signed and dated: *Nattier/p.x. 1754.* Acc. No. 99.1.90.

Elizabeth Hamilton (c. 1720–1800), daughter of a younger son
of the Duke of Hamilton, was married in 1742 to Francis
Greville, later Earl of Warwick. On hearing of their engagement
Horace Walpole wrote, "She is excessively pretty and sensible,
but as diminutive as he." Nattier also painted at least two
portraits of her husband. The composition of the Frick canvas,
simple and restrained, differs markedly from the opulent and
frequently allegorical portraits with which the artist usually
is associated.

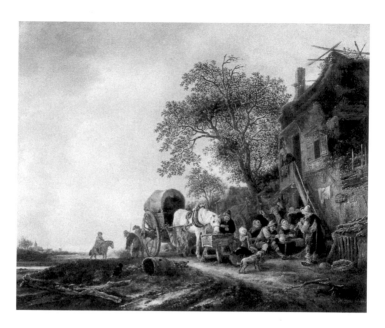

Isack van Ostade 1621-1649

Van Ostade was born in Haarlem and worked there throughout his short career. He studied with his older brother Adriaen, whose scenes of peasant cottages and taverns were the chief inspiration for his early work. A prolific painter, Isack later turned to outdoor genre subjects and winter landscapes.

Travelers Halting at an Inn

Oil, on oak panel, 20⅛ × 24½ in. (51.1 × 62.2 cm.).
Signed: *Isack. Ostade.* Acc. No.07.1.91.

Like his more famous brother and other Haarlem painters, van Ostade was much attracted by the picturesque animation of country inns. He treated aspects of this theme often, typically, as here, in landscapes enriched by subtle effects of silvery daylight.

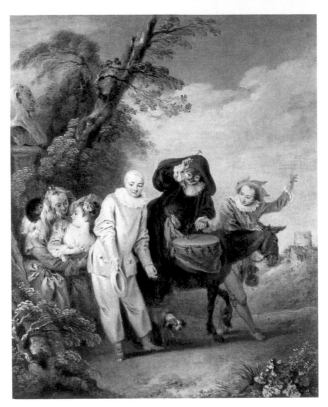

Jean-Baptiste Pater 1695–1736

Born in Valenciennes, Pater received his artistic training from his fellow townsman Jean-Antoine Watteau, whom he accompanied to Paris around 1710. The two later parted because of temperamental differences, but in 1721 Watteau, mortally ill, made peace with Pater, who appears to have inherited his unfinished paintings and some commissions. Pater was elected to the Academy in 1728 as a painter of fêtes galantes.

Procession of Italian Comedians

Oil, on canvas, 29¼ × 23⅜ in. (74.3 × 59.4 cm.).
Acc. No. 18.1.92.

Though this painting and *The Village Orchestra* seem to have been regarded as pendants as early as 1739, they have no precise iconographical relationship. The stock characters who appear in the *Procession*—including from the left Pantaloon, Harlequin, Columbine, Pierrot, the Doctor, and Scapin—recur frequently in the art and literature of Pater's day. They were popularized by the roving troupes of Italian *commedia dell'arte* players who had been banished from France by Louis XIV but returned to enjoy great success after his death.

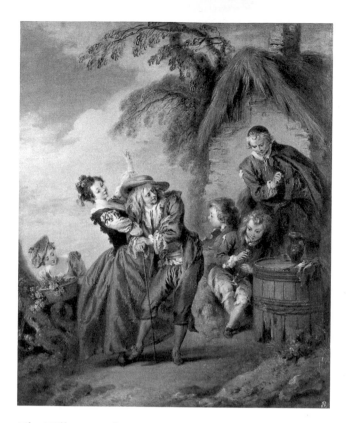

Pater

The Village Orchestra

Oil, on canvas, 29⅜ × 23½ in. (74.6 × 59.7 cm.).
Acc. No. 18.1.93.

In contrast to the theatrical costumes and gestures of the
Procession, The Village Orchestra evokes the daily life of
eighteenth-century France with its depiction of a young
couple in rustic dress dancing to the music of a violin, pipe,
and hurdy-gurdy. The elegant figures and polished technique
that characterize both canvases demonstrate Pater's debt to
his master, Watteau, to whom the paintings once were attributed.

Piero della Francesca 1410/20–1492

Born in the Tuscan town of Borgo Sansepolcro, Piero is first recorded in 1439 working with Domenico Veneziano in Florence. In 1451 he painted a fresco for Sigismondo Malatesta in Rimini, and the following year he began his celebrated fresco cycle of the Legend of the True Cross in the church of S. Francesco at Arezzo. Piero's art reflects his deep interest in the theoretical study of perspective and geometry.

St. Simon the Apostle (?)

Tempera, on poplar panel, 52¾ × 24½ in. (134 × 62.2 cm.).
Painted probably between 1454 and 1469. Acc. No. 36.1.138.

In 1454 Angelo di Giovanni di Simone d'Angelo ordered from Piero a polyptych for the high altar of S. Agostino in Borgo Sansepolcro. The commission specified that this work, undertaken to fulfill the wish of Angelo's late brother Simone and the latter's wife Giovanna for the spiritual benefit of the donors and their forebears, was to consist of several panels with "images, figures, pictures, and ornaments." The central portion of the altarpiece is lost, but four lateral panels with standing saints—St. Simon the Apostle (?), St. Michael the Archangel, St. Augustine, and St. Nicholas of Tolentino—have survived. Though the venerable figure in the Frick painting was given no identifying attributes, he is presumed to represent either St. Simon, patron saint of the deceased brother Simone, or possibly St. John the Evangelist, patron of the donors' father and of Simone's wife. The steps seen at lower left in the Frick panel are probably a continuation of the base of a throne from the missing central section, which may have depicted a Madonna and Child or an Assumption or Coronation of the Virgin. Steps also appear at lower right in the St. Michael panel.

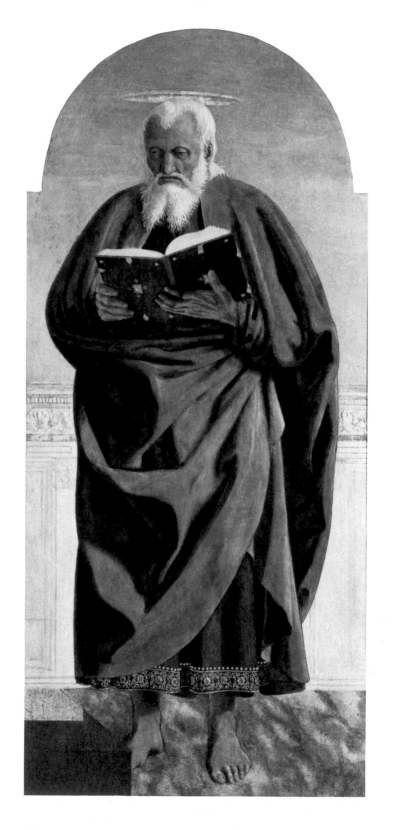

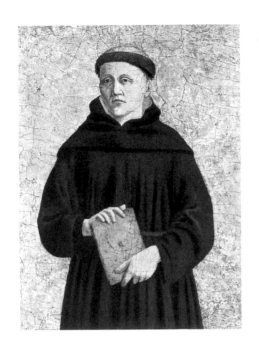 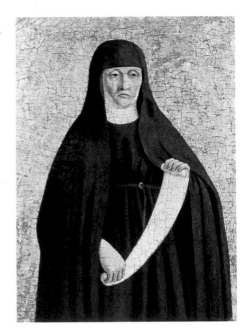

Piero della Francesca, Workshop of

Augustinian Monk
Tempera, on poplar panel, 15¾ × 11⅛ in. (40 × 28.2 cm.).
Acc. No. 50.1.157.

Augustinian Nun
Tempera, on poplar panel, 15¼ × 11 in. (38.7 × 27.9 cm.).
Acc. No. 50.1.158.

First recorded in 1848 at Borgo Sansepolcro, these two panels
and a matching *St. Apollonia* now in the National Gallery,
Washington, are believed to have formed subsidiary parts of
Piero's S. Agostino altarpiece (see preceding entry). Though
the subjects of the Frick panels lack distinctive attributes, it
has been suggested that they may represent the Blessed Angelo
Scarpetti, the most revered local Augustinian monk, who
was buried beneath the high altar of S. Agostino, and
St. Monica, mother of St. Augustine and putative founder of
the order of Augustinian nuns.

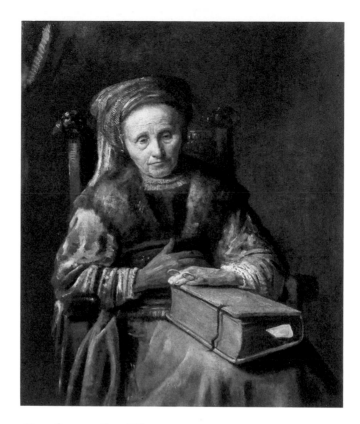

Carel van der Pluym 1625-1672

Van der Pluym was born and lived in Leyden, where his family were official city plumbers and where the young artist became a charter member of the painters' guild in 1648. He was a cousin of Rembrandt, with whom he may have studied and whose style he imitated.

Old Woman with a Book
Oil, on canvas, 38⅝ × 30¾ in. (98.1 × 78.1 cm.).
Acc. No. 16.1.99.

Like many other pictures of old women done in the style of Rembrandt, this canvas was once believed to be a portrait by that artist of his mother. However, the coloring and modeling more closely resemble those of the few signed works by van der Pluym.

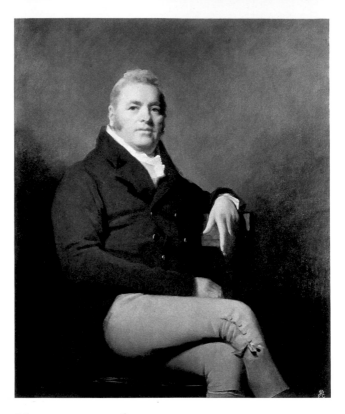

Sir Henry Raeburn 1756–1823

By his early twenties Raeburn had established himself as a painter of portraits and miniatures in his native Edinburgh. From 1785 to 1787 he worked in Rome on the advice of Reynolds, and soon after his return he became the leading portraitist in Scotland. He was elected to the Royal Academy in 1815 and named His Majesty's Limner for Scotland in 1822.

James Cruikshank

Oil, on canvas, 50 × 40 in. (127 × 101.6 cm.). Acc. No. 11.1.94.

James Cruikshank (d. 1830) of Montrose, Forfarshire, was a businessman who made a large fortune from sugar plantations in the British West Indies. No record of the commission for Raeburn's portraits of Cruikshank and his wife has been found, but a dating of between 1805 and 1808 has been suggested on stylistic grounds.

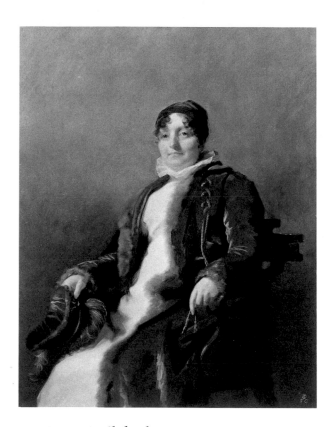

Raeburn

Mrs. James Cruikshank
Oil, on canvas, 50¾ × 40 in. (128.9 × 101.6 cm.).
Acc. No. 05.1.95.

Margaret Helen Gerard, daughter of an Aberdeen minister,
married James Cruikshank in 1792 and died in 1823. Raeburn's
companion portraits of the Cruikshanks were separated for a
number of years before being reunited in Mr. Frick's collection
in 1911.

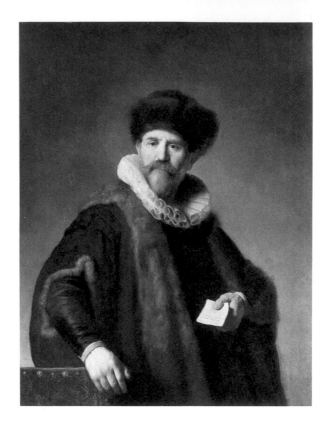

Rembrandt Harmensz. van Rijn 1606–1669

Born in Leyden, Rembrandt studied there and later worked in Amsterdam under Pieter Lastman. Around 1625 he returned to Leyden, where he taught the first of his many pupils, but in 1631/32 he settled permanently in Amsterdam, quickly achieving success as a painter of single and group portraits, Biblical scenes, and historical subjects. He also executed numerous etchings and drawings.

Nicolaes Ruts

Oil, on mahogany panel, 46 × 34⅜ in. (116.8 × 87.3 cm.).
Signed and dated: R[H?]L. 1631. Acc. No. 43.1.150.

Nicolaes Ruts (1573–1638) was an Amsterdam merchant who traded with Russia, the source no doubt of the rich furs he wears in this painting. Perhaps the first portrait commission Rembrandt received from outside his own family, the picture must have contributed to his rapid rise to fame. The dramatic contrasts in lighting and the detailed rendering of the varied textures are characteristic of Rembrandt's early production, differing markedly from the warm, diffused light and broad brushwork that distinguish the Frick *Self-Portrait* painted over a quarter of a century later.

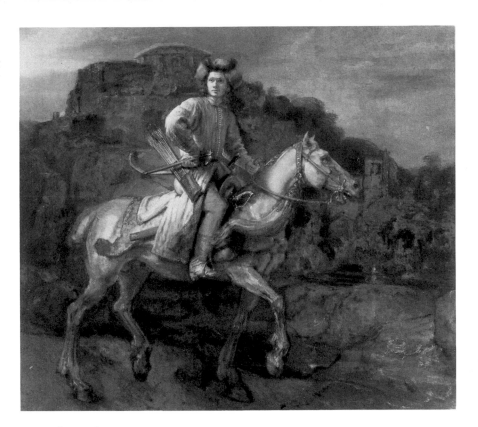

Rembrandt

The Polish Rider
Oil, on canvas, 46 × 53 ⅛ in. (116.8 × 134.9 cm.).
Signed: *R[e?]*. Painted about 1655. Acc. No. 10.1.98.

Ranked among Rembrandt's most impressive and moving
works, this enigmatic depiction of a young warrior riding
resolutely through a shadowy landscape has evoked many
interpretations, all of them inconclusive. It is not a conventional
equestrian portrait, nor does it appear to represent a historical
or literary figure, though a number have been proposed.
Rembrandt may have meant only to portray an exotic horseman,
a popular contemporary theme, or perhaps intended the
painting as a glorification of the latter-day Christian knights
who in his time were still defending eastern Europe from
the advancing Turks.

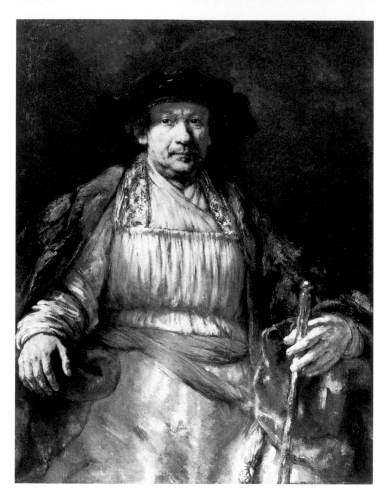

Rembrandt

Self-Portrait
Oil, on canvas, 52⅝ × 40⅞ in. (133.7 × 103.8 cm.).
Signed and dated: *Rembrandt/f. 1658*. Acc. No. 06.1.97.

Rembrandt painted over sixty self-portraits and drew and
etched his likeness repeatedly. These works range from youthful efforts that often served as experiments in dramatic
lighting effects or transitory facial expressions to the more
subtle and searching images of his mature years. The Frick
canvas, with its psychological depth, monumental design,
and rich, warm coloring, is surely the most imposing of these
portraits. The artist, poor and burdened with personal
problems, depicted himself—in poignant and perhaps ironic
contrast—in the splendid costume and enthroned dignity
of an Oriental monarch.

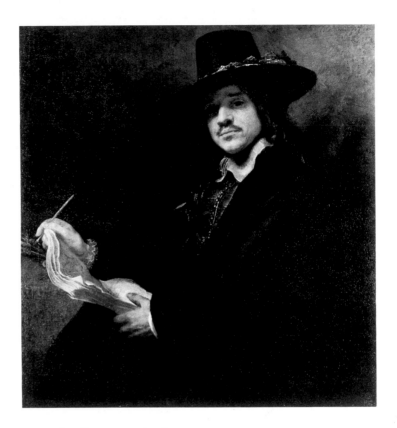

Rembrandt

Portrait of a Young Artist
Oil, on canvas, 39⅛ × 35 in. (99.4 × 88.9 cm.).
Spurious signature and date: *Rembrandt f: | 164[7?]*.
Acc. No. 99.1.96.

The identity of the subject remains in question, though he
has at times been called Leonaert Bramer, Carel Fabritius,
Jan van de Cappelle, and Jan Asselyn. The painting is in the
style of Rembrandt's portraits of the late 1640s, but it could
well be the product of a pupil or imitator. Mr. Frick's purchase
of this canvas in 1899 signaled a new stage in his development
as a collector; previously he had favored the work of
contemporary French Academic and Barbizon painters.

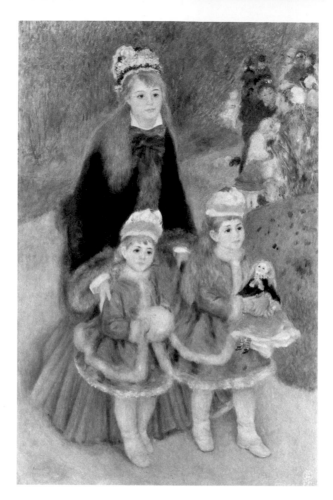

Pierre-Auguste Renoir 1841-1919

Renoir began his career as a painter of porcelain and at twenty-one enrolled in the Paris École des Beaux-Arts. He first showed at the Salon in 1864, and ten years later he took part in the first Impressionist exhibition. After visits to Algeria and Italy in 1881–82 his work began to diverge from that of the Impressionists.

Mother and Children

Oil, on canvas, 67 × 42⅝ in. (170.2 × 108.3 cm.).
Signed: *Renoir*. Painted probably about 1874–76.
Acc. No. 14.1.100.

In 1876 Renoir rented a new studio at the top of Montmartre with funds he had received for a portrait of a mother and her two little girls, very possibly the Frick canvas. Such pleasing portraits brought the artist success at a time when his fellow Impressionists were having difficulty selling their works.

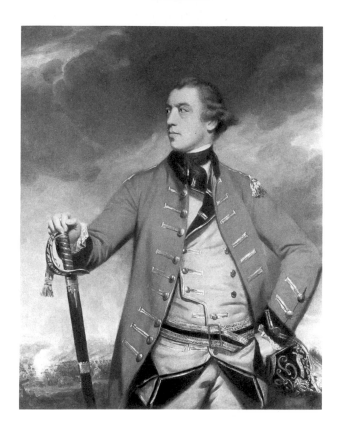

Sir Joshua Reynolds 1723–1792

Reynolds served as apprentice under Thomas Hudson before launching his career in his native Plymouth. Between 1749 and 1752 he was in Italy, where the study of ancient art and the Italian masters profoundly affected his style. Soon after his return he became the most fashionable portraitist in London. As first president of the Royal Academy he delivered a series of "Discourses" that were highly influential in shaping British aesthetic theory.

General John Burgoyne

Oil, on canvas, 50 × 39⅞ in. (127 × 101.3 cm.).
Painted probably in 1766. Acc. No. 43.1.149.

Best remembered as the British commander who in 1777 surrendered to American forces at Saratoga, John Burgoyne (1722–92) was also known in his day as a dandy, gambler, actor, amateur playwright, and Member of Parliament. This portrait may have been commissioned by his senior officer, Count La Lippe, as a memento of their Portugese campaign of 1762. Burgoyne's uniform is that of the Sixteenth Light Dragoons as it was worn until May of 1766.

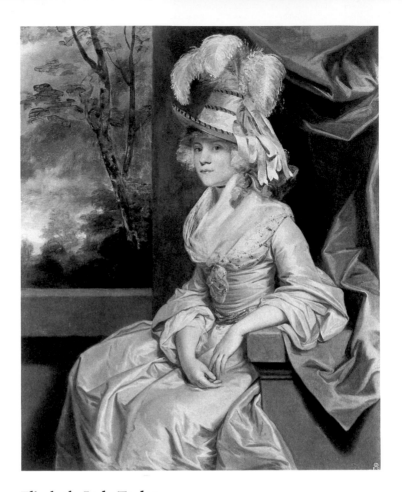

Reynolds

Elizabeth, Lady Taylor

Oil, on canvas, 50⅛ × 40¼ in. (127.3 × 102.2 cm.).
Painted about 1780. Acc. No. 10.1.101.

The subject is thought to have been Elizabeth Goodin Houghton,
who married Sir John Taylor in 1778 and died in 1831.
However, a number of clients named Taylor were painted
by Reynolds, whose abbreviated, often illegible records of
payments make it difficult to identify sitters or to date works
accurately. The dress and tall plumed hat suggest that the
portrait was executed in the late 1770s or early 1780s.

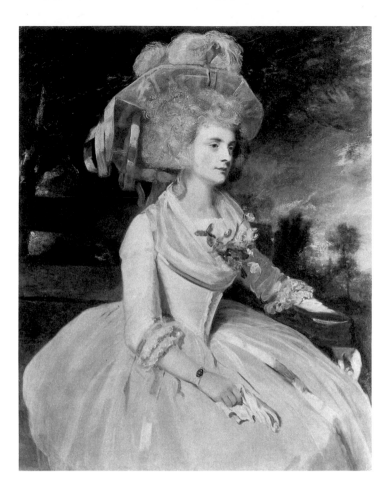

Reynolds

Selina, Lady Skipwith
Oil, on canvas, 50½ × 40¼ in. (128.3 × 102.2 cm.).
Painted in 1787. Acc. No.06.1.102.

Selina Shirley (1752–1832) was married in 1785 to Sir Thomas
George Skipwith of Newbold Hall, Warwickshire. Lady
Skipwith had a reputation as a skilled horsewoman, and a
nephew records that "there was something rather formidable
in her powdered hair and [the] riding habit or joseph which
she generally wore." Reynolds' notebooks show that he
painted her in May of 1787. The natural pose and setting and
fresh, free handling of paint are typical of the artist's late style.

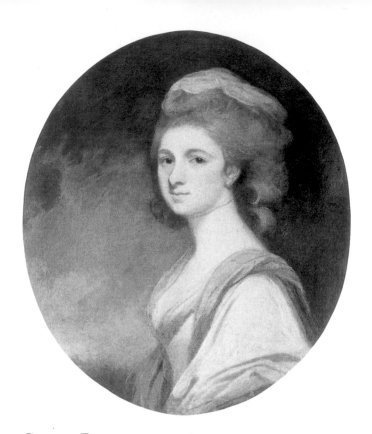

George Romney 1734–1802

*Before moving to London in 1762, Romney had studied and achieved
some success in the north of England. He visited Paris in 1764, and
from 1773 until 1775 he lived in Italy. He was a prolific artist who
rivaled Reynolds as a fashionable portraitist.*

Miss Frances Mary Harford

Oil, on canvas, 30 × 25 ¼ in. (76.2 × 64.1 cm.).
Painted between 1780 and 1783. Acc. No. 03.1.105.

Born about 1759, Frances Harford was the natural daughter of
Frederick Calvert, seventh Lord Baltimore, whose family
had founded the province of Maryland. Bequeathed a large
sum by her father, she was married at thirteen to her guardian,
Robert Morris. After this union was declared void twelve
years later she married the Hon. William Frederick Wyndham,
youngest son of the second Earl of Egremont. The records of
sittings in Romney's diaries indicate that he painted three or
four portraits of Miss Harford.

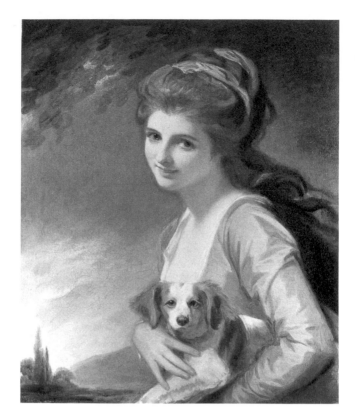

Romney   **Lady Hamilton as 'Nature'**
Oil, on canvas, 29⅞ × 24¾ in. (75.8 × 62.9 cm.).
Painted in 1782. Acc. No. 04.1.103.

Emma Lyon (1765–1815), who later in life called herself Emily
Hart, was the daughter of a Cheshire blacksmith. A fascinating
personality and beauty, she was in turn the mistress of the Hon.
Charles Greville, who commissioned this portrait, of Sir
William Hamilton, Greville's uncle and British envoy to
Naples, whom she married in 1791, and of Lord Nelson, with
whom she lived until his death in 1805. She died in poverty
in Calais. At the height of her social success Lady Hamilton
was famous for her "attitudes"—a kind of romantic aesthetic
posturing. Romney painted more than twenty portraits of
his "divine lady," many in the guise of characters from history,
mythology, and literature.

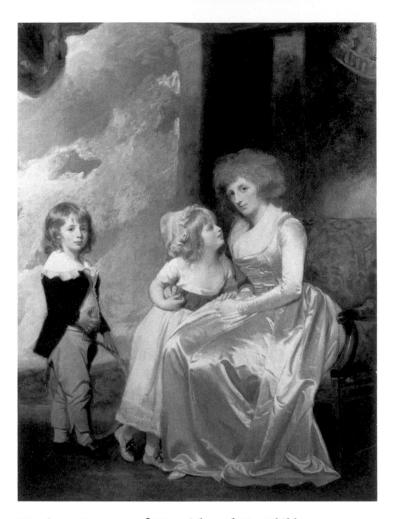

Romney

Henrietta, Countess of Warwick, and Her Children
Oil, on canvas, 79¾ × 61½ in. (202.6 × 156.2 cm.).
Painted 1787–89. Acc. No. 08.1.107.

Henrietta Vernon (1760–1838), daughter of Richard Vernon, the so-called Father of the Turf, became at sixteen the second wife of George Greville, Earl of Warwick. Horace Walpole mentioned her and her sisters in his letters and also wrote verses to them. Romney has depicted her with two of her children, presumably Henry Richard and Elizabeth, in a composition that recalls the group portraits Van Dyck painted in England.

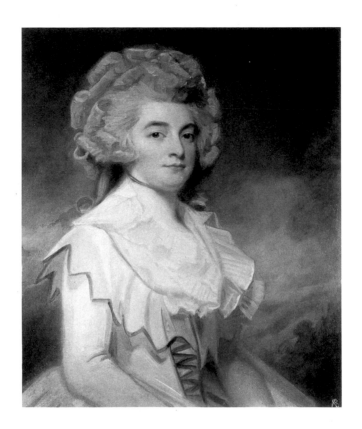

Romney

Miss Mary Finch–Hatton
Oil, on canvas, 29⅞ × 25⅛ in. (75.8 × 63.8 cm.).
Painted in 1788. Acc. No.98.1.104.

Mary Finch-Hatton, daughter of John Finch-Hatton of
Long Stanton Hall, near Cambridge, married Hale Wortham
of Royston, Hertfordshire. Romney's notebooks record six
sittings for this portrait of her, which in its bold and summary
brushwork resembles the technique of the artist's numerous
wash drawings.

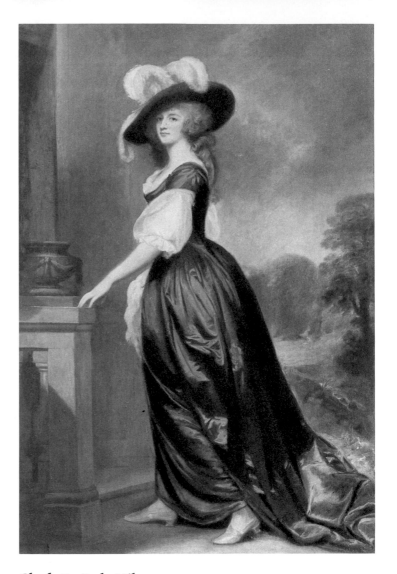

Romney

Charlotte, Lady Milnes
Oil, on canvas, 95⅛ × 58¾ in. (241.6 × 149.2 cm.).
Painted 1788–92. Acc. No. 11.1.106.

Charlotte Frances Bentinck (1767/68–1850) was married
in 1785 to Robert Shore Milnes, who ten years later became
Governor of Martinique and in 1798 was named Lieutenant-
Governor of Lower Canada. Milnes, a longtime patron of
Romney, commissioned this rather classicizing portrait in 1788,
along with one of himself now at Helperby, Yorkshire.

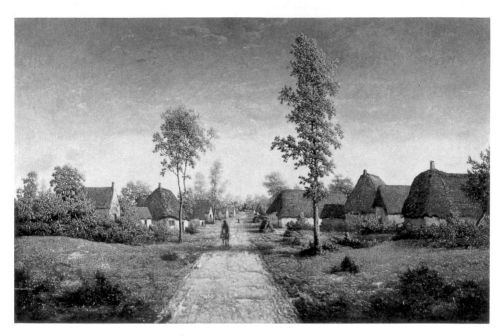

Pierre-Étienne-Théodore Rousseau 1812–1867

Rousseau was born and trained in Paris, where he was much influenced by the Dutch landscapes in the Louvre. He began exhibiting at the Salon in 1831 but had little success until 1849, when he won a first-class medal and considerable public acclaim. After the Revolution of 1848 he settled in the village of Barbizon with Millet, Daubigny, and others of the group that came to be known as the Barbizon school.

The Village of Becquigny
Oil, on mahogany panel, 25 × 39⅜ in. (63.5 × 100 cm.).
Signed: *TH. Rousseau*. Begun about 1857. Acc. No. 02.1.108.

During his last ten years Rousseau frequently revised this panel representing a village in Picardy, a composition that clearly recalls seventeenth-century Dutch landscapes. The day before sending the picture to the Salon of 1864 he altered the sky to a bright sapphire blue, in imitation of the first Japanese prints he had seen, but the color was so widely criticized that he later restored the original softer hues. The artist's friends considered this one of his most important and successful achievements.

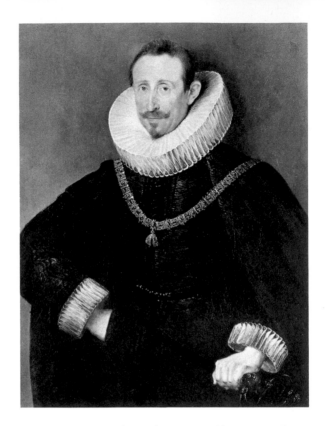

Sir Peter Paul Rubens, Follower of
Seventeenth Century

Rubens (1577–1640) worked in Italy, Spain, England, and France as well as in his native Flanders, where he directed a large workshop employing numerous assistants. His style influenced many of his contemporaries throughout Europe.

A Knight of the Order of the Golden Fleece
Oil, on canvas, 39¾ × 30½ in. (101 × 77.5 cm.).
Acc. No. 15.1.109.

Once ascribed to Rubens himself, this work has since been assigned, with insufficient evidence, to various of his collaborators, including Van Dyck, Snyders, and Cornelis de Vos. A version in the New York Historical Society, attributed to de Vos, is identified as a portrait of Ambrogio Spinola, who was commander of Spanish forces in the Netherlands and a friend of Rubens. A copy of the portrait, or of its prototype, by Chassériau is implausibly said to represent Don Fernando Álvarez de Toledo, third Duke of Alba, who was Spanish Viceroy of the Netherlands and died in 1582.

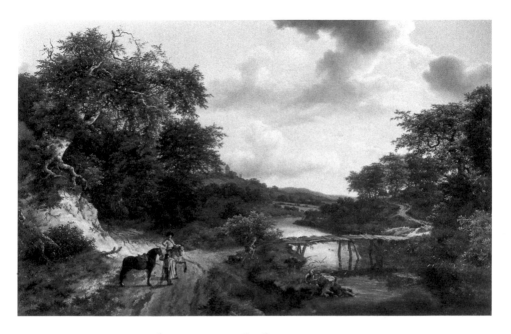

Jacob van Ruisdael 1628/29–1682

Ruisdael was born in Haarlem and entered the painters' guild there in 1648, presumably after studying with his uncle Salomon van Ruysdael. By 1657 he was living in Amsterdam, where he seems to have spent the rest of his life. His many paintings, drawings, and etchings are devoted entirely to landscape.

Landscape with a Footbridge

Oil, on canvas, 38¾ × 62⅝ in. (98.4 × 159.1 cm.).
Signed and dated: *JRuisdael 1652.* Acc. No.49.1.156.

In 1650 Ruisdael traveled to the province of Overijssel near the Dutch-German frontier and made drawings there of hilly scenery that differs markedly from the flat countryside of western Holland, the chief subject of the earlier Haarlem landscapists. In this painting, completed two years later, the youthful artist demonstrates his special gift for rendering subtle effects of light, evident in the pale sun that filters through the clouds to dapple the landscape and reflect from the surface of the stream.

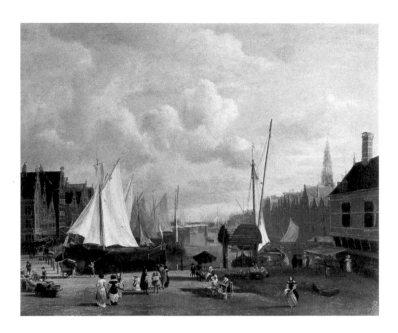

Ruisdael

Quay at Amsterdam
Oil, on canvas, 20⅜ × 25⅞ in. (51.7 × 65.7 cm.).
Signed: *JRuisdael*. Painted about 1670. Acc. No. 10.1.110.

This rare urban scene by Ruisdael shows in the foreground
the north end of the Dam, the main square of Amsterdam,
and beyond it the broad canal called the Damrak (now filled in).
Among the recognizable buildings is the fourteenth-century
Oude Kerk, whose tower, altered in 1565, rises at right.
Ruisdael painted several views of the square, where he had a
studio in his later years.

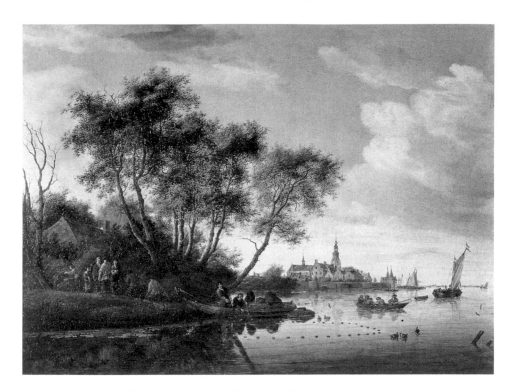

Salomon van Ruysdael 1600 (?)–1670

Ruysdael, an early exponent of the Dutch realist landscape tradition, was born in Naarden, near Amsterdam. In 1623 he became a member of the painters' guild in Haarlem, where he remained until his death. He probably was the teacher of his more celebrated nephew Jacob van Ruisdael.

River Scene: Men Dragging a Net
Oil, on canvas, 26¼ × 35⅛ in. (66.7 × 89.2 cm.).
Painted about 1667. Acc. No.05.1.111.

The town in the background has been identified on the basis of its church and twin-towered gate as Weesp, a community on the Vecht not far from Amsterdam. A riverbank, large trees, fishermen, boats, and distant buildings are motifs that Ruysdael varied and rearranged repeatedly throughout his career. Here they are combined with particularly fine effects of sunset reflected from water.

133

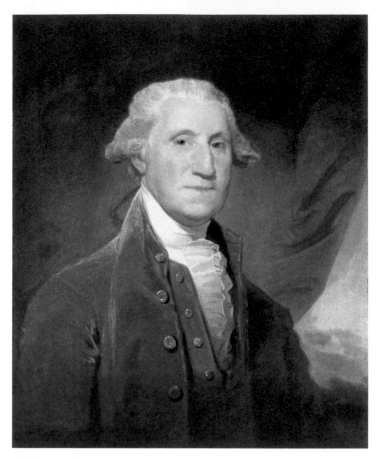

Gilbert Stuart 1755–1828

Stuart was born in North Kingstown, Rhode Island. After studying in Scotland and working in London under his compatriot Benjamin West, he returned in the early 1790s to become the leading American portraitist of his day. He painted chiefly in New York, Philadelphia, and Boston.

George Washington

Oil, on canvas, 29¼ × 24 in. (74.3 × 60.9 cm.).
Painted 1795–96. Acc. No. 18.1.112.

Stuart earned a fortune producing replicas of the three portraits he painted from life of the first United States President. The Frick canvas is thought to be a copy the artist made for John Vaughan of Philadelphia and belongs to the group known as the "Vaughan type," though it differs from the related versions in the color of the coat and the treatment of the background. Stylistically the portrait recalls the work of Stuart's English contemporaries, such as Romney and Hoppner.

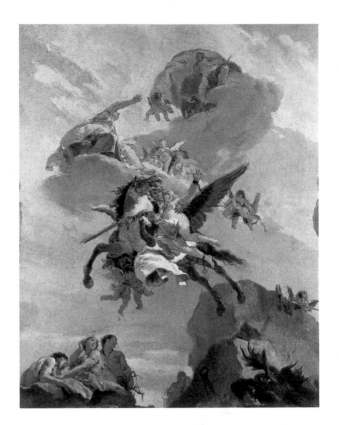

Giovanni Battista Tiepolo 1696–1770

Tiepolo's brilliant talents, especially as a decorator of palaces, villas, and churches, won him fame far beyond his native Venice.
He worked for patrons throughout North Italy and received major commissions from Würzburg and Madrid. A prolific artist, he produced religious, historical, and mythological paintings as well as numerous drawings and etchings.

Perseus and Andromeda

Oil, on paper affixed to canvas, 20⅜ × 16 in. (51.8 × 40.6 cm.).
Painted probably in 1730. Acc. No. 18.1.114.

In Greek myth, the Ethiopian princess Andromeda was chained to a rock by her father as sacrifice to a sea monster sent to ravage his kingdom. Her rescue by Perseus astride Pegasus is the subject of this oil sketch, a study for a ceiling fresco in the Palazzo Archinto, Milan (destroyed by bombing in 1943). The figures, illusionistically conceived to be seen from below, soar upward toward the gold-tinged heavens, where Minerva and Jupiter discuss their fate.

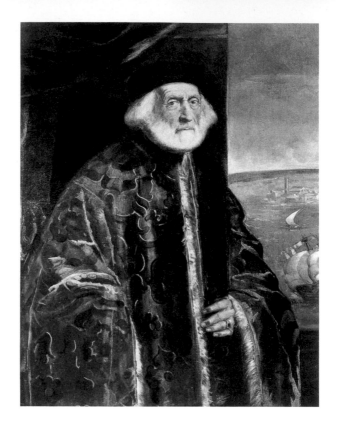

Jacopo Tintoretto, Circle of

Jacopo Robusti (1518–94), called Il Tintoretto, is best known for the religious paintings he produced for Venetian churches and confraternities, but he also executed portraits and mythological and allegorical cycles. His large workshop included his sons Domenico and Marco and daughter Marietta, who along with others perpetuated his style well into the seventeenth century.

Portrait of a Venetian Procurator

Oil, on canvas, 44⅝ × 35 in. (113.3 × 88.9 cm.).
Acc. No. 38.1.142.

The crimson robes and black cap and stole worn by the unknown subject of this portrait identify him as a Procurator of St. Mark, a high Venetian official with administrative and charitable duties and a seat in the Senate. Since the distant view of the island of S. Giorgio Maggiore at right does not include Palladio's church of S. Giorgio, the cornerstone of which was laid in 1566, the portrait or its prototype presumably was painted before that date.

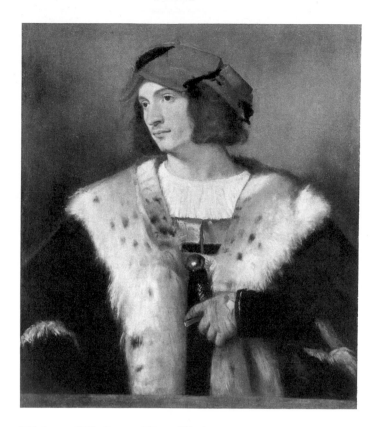

Titian (Tiziano Vecellio) 1477/90-1576

Titian was born in the Alpine town of Pieve di Cadore; the date of his birth is uncertain. He succeeded Giovanni Bellini, under whom he had studied, as painter to the Republic of Venice, and he included among his many illustrious patrons the Emperor Charles V, Charles' son Philip II of Spain, and Pope Paul III. He died in Venice in the great plague of 1576.

Portrait of a Man in a Red Cap
Oil, on canvas, 32⅜ × 28 in. (82.3 × 71.1 cm.).
Painted about 1516. Acc. No. 15.1.116.

This portrait of a richly dressed young man is generally considered an early work of Titian. The contemplative mood of the subject and the diffused, gentle play of light over broadly painted surfaces are strongly reminiscent of Titian's Venetian contemporary Giorgione, to whom the canvas has in the past been attributed.

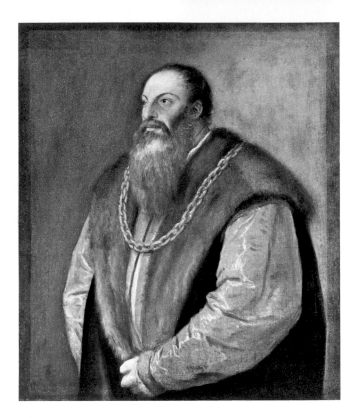

Titian

Pietro Aretino
Oil, on canvas, 40⅛ × 33¾ in. (102 × 85.7 cm.).
Painted probably between 1548 and the early 1550s.
Acc. No. 05.1.115.

Pietro Aretino (1492–1556), author of scurrilous verses, lives
of saints, comedies, tragedies, and innumerable letters, also
attained considerable wealth and influence through literary
flattery and blackmail. He was on intimate terms with Titian,
who painted at least three portraits of him. Here the artist
conveys a sense of his friend's intellectual power through the
keen, forceful head and of his worldliness through the solid,
rounded mass of the richly robed figure.

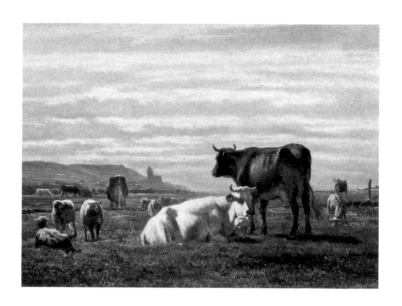

Constant Troyon 1810–1865

The son of a painter at the Sèvres porcelain works, Troyon received his first lessons from the factory manager. He later became associated with Rousseau, Dupré, and others of the Barbizon group. A prize awarded him in 1846 made possible a visit to Holland, where he was much influenced by the Dutch landscapists, especially Cuyp and Potter.

A Pasture in Normandy

Oil, on panel, 17 × 25⅝ in. (43.2 × 65.1 cm.).
Signed: C. TROYON. Painted in the 1850s. Acc. No. 99.1.117.

At the insistence of his friends, Troyon began in the 1840s adding to his landscapes the figures of animals he had sketched in barns when inclement weather prevented him from working outdoors. By 1855 he was well known throughout Europe not only as a landscape painter but particularly as an *animalier*. The background in the Frick picture appears again, viewed from a slightly different angle, in two other Troyon compositions.

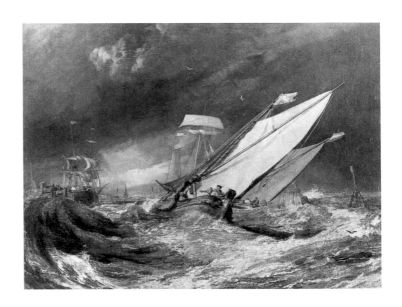

Joseph Mallord William Turner 1775–1851

Turner, the son of a London barber, studied at the Royal Academy, to which he was granted full membership at the age of twenty-seven. Known initially as a watercolorist, he began exhibiting oils in the mid-1790s. He traveled extensively in England and on the Continent and made innumerable sketches, many of which he used as the basis for paintings and prints.

Fishing Boats Entering Calais Harbor
Oil, on canvas, 29 × 38¾ in. (73.7 × 98.4 cm.).
Painted about 1803. Acc. No.04.1.120.

In July of 1802, during the temporary Peace of Amiens, Turner began his first visit to the Continent. He recorded his arrival at Calais in several sketches, which he later worked up into this canvas and the much larger *Calais Pier* now in the National Gallery, London. The churning waters and stormy skies in both works recall Dutch seascapes of the seventeenth century.

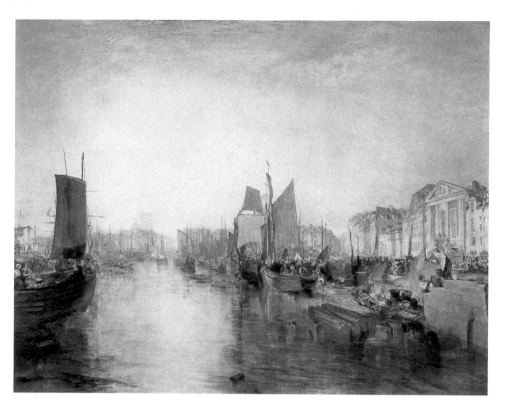

Turner

The Harbor of Dieppe
Oil, on canvas, 68⅜ × 88¾ in. (173.7 × 225.4 cm.).
Dated: *182[6?]*. Acc. No. 14.1.122.

Dieppe is one of several large exhibition pieces Turner
painted representing northern Continental ports (see also
following entry). Sketches for it date from the late summer
of 1821 and record a number of buildings that still stand.
The intense luminosity of the painting displeased many
contemporary critics, one of whom called it a "splendid
piece of falsehood." Another, however, wrote, "Not even
Claude in his happiest efforts, has exceeded the brilliant
composition before us."

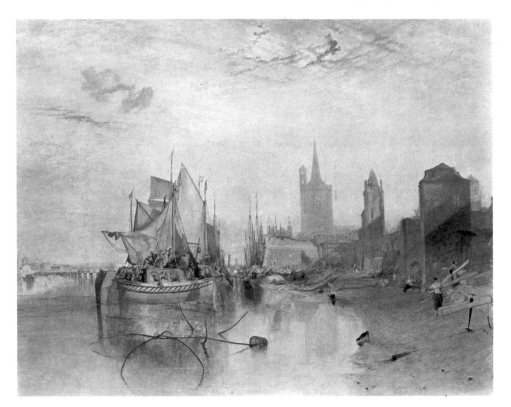

Turner

Cologne: The Arrival of a Packet-Boat: Evening
Oil, and possibly watercolor, on canvas, 66⅜ × 88¼ in.
(168.6 × 224.1 cm.). Painted in 1826. Acc. No. 14.1.119.

According to an account of Ruskin's, Turner quixotically
covered the golden sky of this painting with a wash of lamp-
black during the Royal Academy exhibition of 1826 in order
not to detract from two portraits by Lawrence that hung to
either side of it. However, contemporary critical references
to its "glitter and gaud of colors" as well as to the delicate
nature of its surface medium cast doubt on Ruskin's anecdote.
The composition is based on sketches Turner made while
touring the Rhine in 1817 and again in 1825.

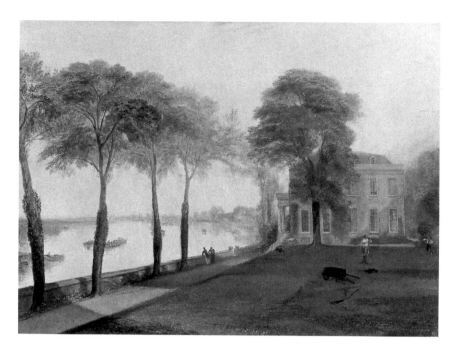

Turner

Mortlake Terrace: Early Summer Morning
Oil, on canvas, 36⅝ × 48½ in. (93 × 123.2 cm.).
Painted in 1826. Acc. No.09.1.121.

This canvas painted for William Moffatt depicts Moffatt's
estate at Mortlake, on the Thames just west of London.
Like so many of Turner's works, it is based on numerous
preparatory drawings, in which the artist recorded the
topography and studied various ways of balancing the mass
of the house and land against the open river and sky.
A companion view of the terrace and river on a summer
evening as seen from a ground-floor window of the house is
in the National Gallery, Washington.

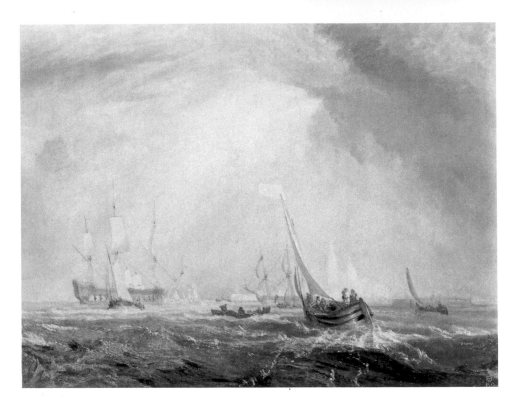

Turner

Antwerp: Van Goyen Looking Out for a Subject
Oil, on canvas, 36⅛ × 48⅜ in. (91.8 × 122.9 cm.).
Painted in 1833. Acc. No.01.1.118.

The reference in the painting's title and the inscription VAN G
on the stern of the nearest boat identify the turbaned figure
standing in that vessel as the Dutch landscapist Jan van Goyen.
Like Turner, van Goyen visited Antwerp and executed
paintings based on sketches done there. This allusion to a
seventeenth-century Dutch painter is not unique in Turner's
titles—witness his *Rembrandt's Daughter* and *Port Ruysdael*.

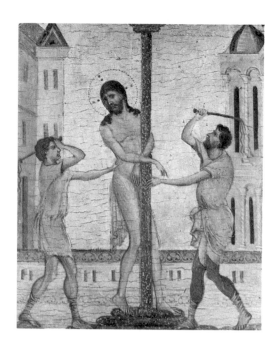

Tuscan School Late Thirteenth Century (?)

The Flagellation of Christ

Tempera, on poplar panel, 9¾ × 7⅞ in. (24.7 × 20 cm.).
Acc. No. 50.1.159.

This small panel, no doubt originally part of an altarpiece
or tabernacle, has provoked considerable scholarly debate,
eliciting attributions to Duccio, to Cimabue, and to an unknown
Tuscan artist influenced by both. The subject of the Flagel-
lation acquired particular importance during the second half
of the thirteenth century, not only in painting but also in
religious poetry and drama. Those same years saw great pil-
grimages of penitents who, in imitation of Christ's suffering,
lashed themselves and one another as they marched in procession
through the countryside.

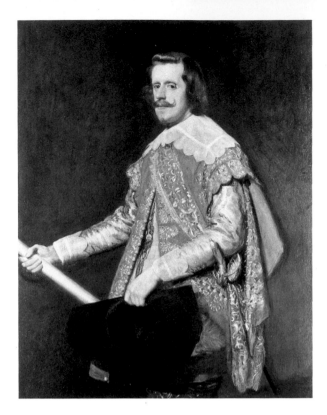

Diego Rodríguez de Silva y Velázquez 1599–1660

Velázquez was born in Seville and apprenticed there to Francisco Pacheco. In 1623 he entered the service of Philip IV, to whom he became both official painter and personal friend. Apart from visits to Italy in 1629–31 and 1649–51, he remained at the Spanish court until his death.

King Philip IV of Spain
Oil, on canvas, 51⅛ × 39⅛ in. (129.8 × 99.4 cm.).
Painted in 1644. Acc. No. 11.1.123.

Philip IV (1605–65), who succeeded to the throne in 1621, was a weak ruler but a lavish patron of the arts and letters. He promoted the Spanish theater, built the Palacio del Buen-Retiro at Madrid, enlarged the Royal collections, and was Velázquez' most ardent supporter. In 1644 Velázquez accompanied the King to Fraga, where on May 15 the Spaniards won an important victory over the French. There, in a dilapidated, makeshift studio, Philip posed for this portrait dressed in the silver-and-rose costume he wore during the campaign.

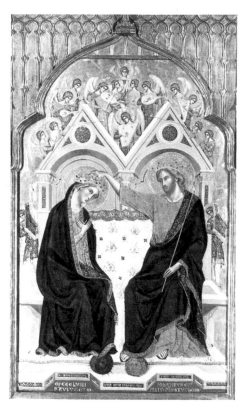

Paolo and Giovanni Veneziano
Paolo, Active 1321–1358

Paolo Veneziano is considered the leading figure of Venetian trecento painting. Little is known of his son Giovanni beyond his participation in the Frick panel and in the painted cover, dated 1345, for the Pala d'Oro in St. Mark's, Venice.

The Coronation of the Virgin

Tempera, on poplar panel, 43 ¼ × 27 in. (110 × 68.5 cm.). Signed and dated: M.C.C.C.L.V.I.I.I. / PAVLVS CVM / IOHANINVS EIV̄ / FILIV̄ / P̄ISERV̄T HOC OP. Acc. No. 30.1.124.

The Coronation of the Virgin is recounted not in the New Testament but in the apocryphal story of the Virgin's death. In many Coronation scenes painted by Paolo and other Venetian artists a sun and a moon accompany the principal figures, the sun from early times being associated with Christ and the moon with the Virgin. The angels singing and playing musical instruments in the Frick panel symbolize the harmony of the universe; their instruments are the authentic components of a medieval orchestra, accurately depicted and correctly held and played.

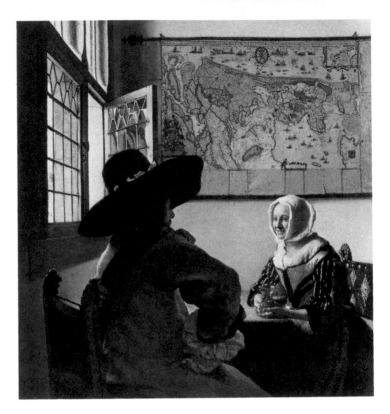

Johannes Vermeer 1632–1675

Vermeer seems to have spent his whole life in Delft, where he joined the painters' guild in 1653. His work shows the influence of Carel Fabritius, who may have been his teacher, and of the Caravaggesque painters of Utrecht. Though his pictures apparently commanded high prices, he produced relatively few; only thirty-five to forty paintings are generally recognized as from his hand.

Officer and Laughing Girl

Oil, on canvas, 19⅞ × 18⅛ in. (50.5 × 46 cm.).
Painted probably about 1655–60. Acc. No. 11.1.127.

In what may be one of the first works of his mature style, Vermeer transforms the theme of a girl entertaining her suitor, already popular in Dutch art, into a dazzling study of light-filled space. The dark foil of the officer's silhouette dramatizes both the illusion of depth and the brilliant play of light over the woman and the furnishings of the chamber. The map of Holland on the far wall, first published in 1621, also appears in two other paintings by Vermeer.

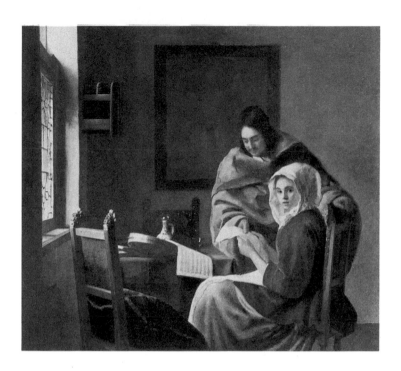

Vermeer

Girl Interrupted at Her Music
Oil, on canvas, 15½ × 17½ in. (39.3 × 44.4 cm.).
Painted about 1660. Acc. No.01.1.125.

Music-making, a recurring subject in Vermeer's interior
scenes, was associated in the seventeenth century with court-
ship. In this painting of a duet or music lesson momentarily
interrupted, the amorous theme is reinforced by the picture
of Cupid with raised left arm dimly visible in the background;
the motif is derived from a popular book on emblems of love
published in 1608 and symbolizes fidelity to a single lover.
Vermeer's treatment of light, space, and the relationship
between the two figures is subtler and more complex here
than in the *Officer and Laughing Girl,* which probably dates
from a few years earlier.

Vermeer

Mistress and Maid
Oil, on canvas, 35 ½ × 31 in. (90.2 × 78.7 cm.).
Painted probably about 1665–70. Acc. No. 19.1.126.

The lack of final modeling in the mistress' head and figure
indicates that this late work by Vermeer was left unfinished.
Nevertheless, the artist seldom if ever surpassed the subtly varied
effects of light seen here as it gleams from the pearl jewelry,
sparkles from the glass and silver objects on the table, and falls
softly over the figures in their shadowy setting. Exceptional
too is the sense of dramatic tension expressed by the two women
arrested in some moment of mysterious crisis. Bought by
Mr. Frick in 1919, the year of his death, this painting was his
last purchase and joined Rembrandt's *Self-Portrait,* Holbein's
Sir Thomas More, Bellini's *St. Francis,* and Velázquez' *King
Philip IV* among his favorite acquisitions.

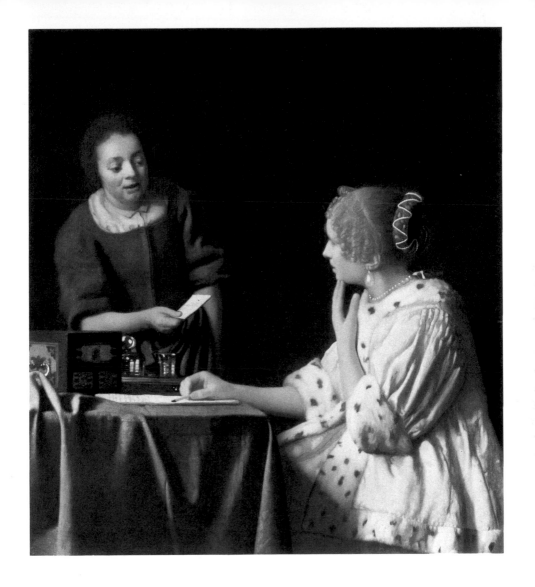

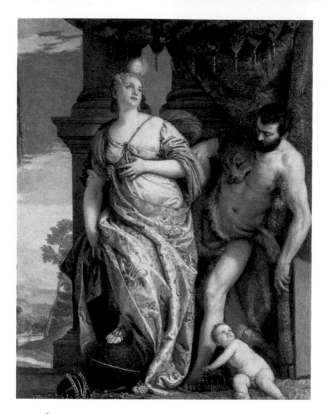

Paolo Veronese c. 1528–1588

*Paolo Caliari was called Il Veronese after his birthplace, Verona.
A master of color, illusionism, and pageantry, he painted monumental
religious, mythological, and allegorical works as well as
magnificent decorations for the villas of patrician families. Except
for a visit to Rome about 1560 he passed most of his mature life in and
around Venice.*

Allegory of Wisdom and Strength
Oil, on canvas, 84½ × 65¾ in. (214.6 × 167 cm.).
Acc. No. 12.1.128.

Veronese expresses the moralizing theme of this picture in
sumptuous style. The female figure gazing heavenward seems
intended to represent Divine Wisdom, with the traditional
attribute of a sun over her head. The shadowed Hercules,
his gaze fixed on the riches strewn over the ground, would
appear here to symbolize earthly power or brute force.
The inscription OMNIA VANITAS (All is Vanity) at lower left is
the keynote of the Book of Ecclesiastes, which stresses the
supremacy of divine wisdom over worldly things and the
labors that produce them.

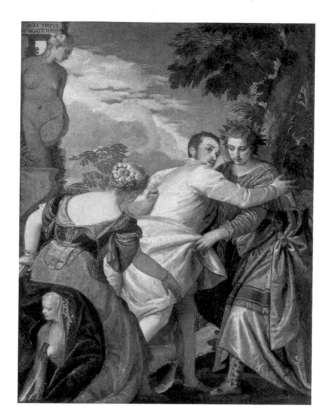

Veronese

Allegory of Virtue and Vice (The Choice of Hercules)
Oil, on canvas, 86¼ × 66¾ in. (219 × 169.5 cm.).
Acc. No. 12.1.129.

The theme of the Choice of Hercules was highly popular in
Renaissance art and literature. According to the legend, the
young hero, finding himself at a crossroads, resists the entice-
ments of Vice, who indicates a path of ease and pleasure, and
follows instead Virtue, who offers a rugged lifelong ascent
that will ultimately lead to true happiness. The motto on the
entablature, [HO]NOR ET VIRTVS / [P]OST MORTĒ FLORET
(Honor and Virtue Flourish after Death), reinforces the moral
significance of the subject. Because of Hercules' distinctive
physiognomy and elegant sixteenth-century costume, this
picture has sometimes been considered an allegorizing portrait,
perhaps of the artist.

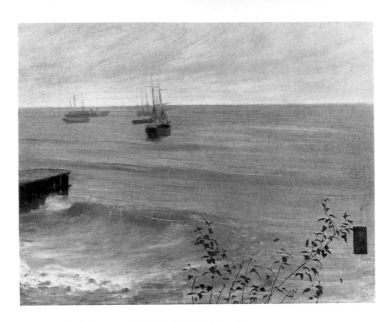

James Abbott McNeill Whistler 1834–1903

Born in Lowell, Massachusetts, Whistler spent part of his childhood and most of his mature life in Europe. After three years at the West Point Military Academy, he went to London and then Paris. He exhibited in the Salon des Refusés in 1863, and throughout his career he associated with his more experimental contemporaries. His wit as well as his advanced style of painting involved him in many lively controversies.

The Ocean

Oil, on canvas, 31¾ × 40⅛ in. (80.7 × 101.9 cm.).
Signed with the butterfly monogram. Painted in 1866.
Acc. No. 14.1.135.

This painting, exhibited in London in 1892 as *Symphony in Grey and Green: The Ocean,* was one of several seascapes Whistler painted in 1866 during a visit to Valparaiso, Chile. The influence of Japanese prints on his work is apparent here in the high horizon, the decorative arrangement of bamboo sprays, and the signature label at lower right. Both picture and frame—the latter designed by the artist himself—bear Whistler's characteristic butterfly monogram.

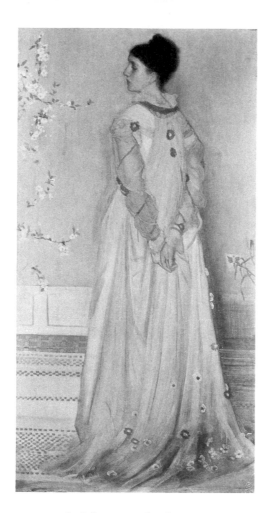

Whistler

Mrs. Frederick R. Leyland
Oil, on canvas, 77⅛ × 40¼ in. (195.9 × 102.2 cm.).
Signed with the butterfly monogram. Painted 1872–73.
Acc. No. 16.1.133.

Frances Dawson (1834–1910) was the wife of Frederick
R. Leyland, a Liverpool shipowner who was one of Whistler's
chief patrons before they quarreled bitterly. The artist painted
the famous Peacock Room now in the Freer Gallery,
Washington, for the Leyland's London home. The Frick
portrait, originally entitled *Symphony in Flesh Colour and Pink,*
apparently was never completely finished. Most of the surviving
preparatory drawings are studies for Mrs. Leyland's gown,
which Whistler designed.

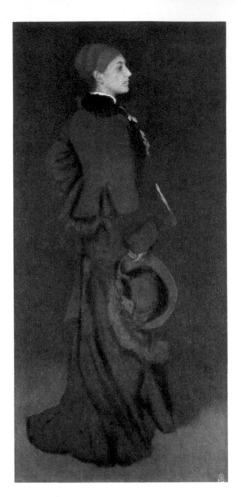

Whistler

Miss Rosa Corder
Oil, on canvas, 75¾ × 36⅜ in. (192.4 × 92.4 cm.).
Painted 1875–78. Acc. No. 14.1.134.

Rosa Corder was a painter and the mistress of Whistler's
unofficial agent, Charles Howell. It is said that Whistler
observed her in Chelsea one day wearing a brown dress and
passing before a black door and, struck by the color effect,
used it as the basis for this portrait, originally called *Arrangement
in Black and Brown*. Miss Corder later reported that she had
posed for the picture some forty times. An acquaintance
remembered her as a person of "a beautiful stillness."

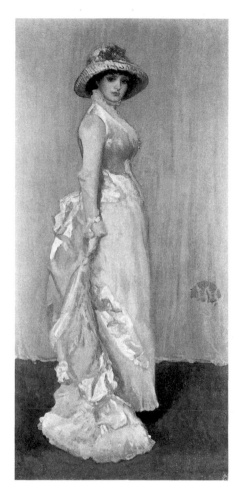

Whistler

Valerie, Lady Meux
Oil, on canvas, 76¼ × 36⅝ in. (193.7 × 93 cm.).
Signed with the butterfly monogram. Painted in 1881.
Acc. No. 18.1.132.

Valerie Susie Reece (c. 1856–1910), daughter of a stage
carpenter at the Drury Lane Theatre, married Sir Henry
Bruce Meux, Bart., a brewer. A colorful figure in society,
she once created a sensation by appearing at a hunt riding an
elephant. This is the second of three portraits Whistler made
of her and was originally called *Harmony in Pink and Gray*.
The first portrait, *Arrangement in Black and White*, is in the
Honolulu Academy of Arts, and the third apparently
was destroyed by the artist before it was completed as the
result of a quarrel with the subject.

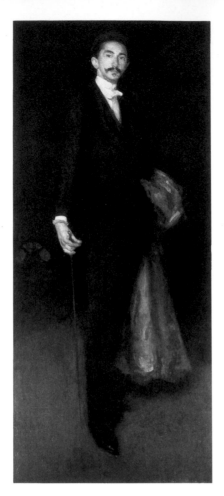

Whistler

Robert, Comte de Montesquiou-Fezensac
Oil, on canvas, 82⅛ × 36⅛ in. (208.6 × 91.8 cm.).
Signed with the butterfly monogram. Painted 1891–92.
Acc. No. 14.1.131.

Robert, Comte de Montesquiou-Fezensac (1855–1921),
was a prominent figure in the social and intellectual world of
Paris around 1900. Though he published numerous volumes
of poetry, he is probably best remembered as one of the models
for the character of Baron de Charlus in Proust's *Remembrance
of Things Past*. Whistler, who received as partial payment
for this portrait an Empire bed presented to Montesquiou's
ancestors by Napoleon, quoted the delighted subject as
exclaiming before the finished work, "It is the acme of pride."

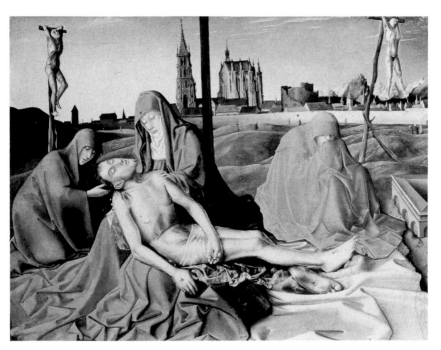

Konrad Witz, Follower of Fifteenth Century

Witz (c. 1400–47) was born in Germany. Though he spent his active years in Switzerland, his influence was widespread and may be traced south of the Alps as well as in the North.

Pietà

Tempera and oil, on panel, 13⅛ × 17½ in.
(33.3 × 44.4 cm.). Acc. No. 81.1.172.

This *Pietà* evidently was the model for a variant, also in The Frick Collection (see p. 65), by a later artist who added a kneeling donor to the composition. Both paintings— individually and in their relation to each other—present many unsolved mysteries. The national origins of the two artists, the patrons who commissioned the panels, and the locations in

which the works were executed are all unknown. North
European characteristics seem stronger in the present, earlier
version, which was long attributed to Konrad Witz.

This *Pietà* is more dramatically intense, more emotional in
the handling of the sharp-featured faces, the angular drapery
folds, and the colder tonality of colors and light. However, the
softer, mellower style of the *Pietà with Donor* results partly
from factors other than geographical origin, such as its more
abraded condition and the fundamental differences between
copying and creating an image. During the fifteenth century,
artists of many nationalities travelled about to courts and
towns throughout Europe, from Provence to Naples, from the
Netherlands to Spain, blending in their works local and
imported traditions. The authors of one or both of the Frick
Pietàs may have been such itinerant artists, whose careers
perhaps crossed at some unidentified cultural center of the
mid-fifteenth century.

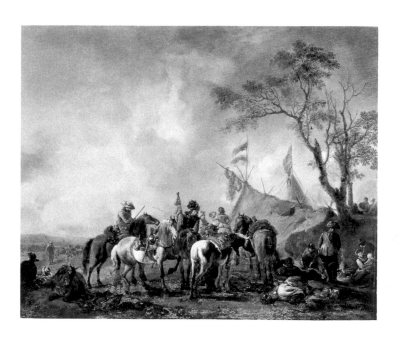

Philips Wouwerman 1619–1668

Wouwerman was born in Haarlem, where he joined the painters'
guild in 1640. His style was evidently much influenced by the genre
paintings of his fellow townsman Pieter van Laer, called Il Bamboccio.
Wouwerman's work was popular in his own time, but the height
of his reputation came during the eighteenth and nineteenth centuries.

The Cavalry Camp
Oil, on oak panel, 16¾ × 20¾ in. (42.5 × 52.7 cm.).
Acc. No.01.1.136.

Though Wouwerman appears to have spent most of his life
in Haarlem, his numerous depictions of army battles suggest
that he may have observed Dutch border campaigns or
traveled abroad. His subtle sense of color and texture is evident
in this composition, which anticipates the tastes of the eighteenth
century. Watteau's early military scenes in particular seem to
depend from precedents such as this.

Giovanni Bellini, *St. Francis in the Desert* (detail)

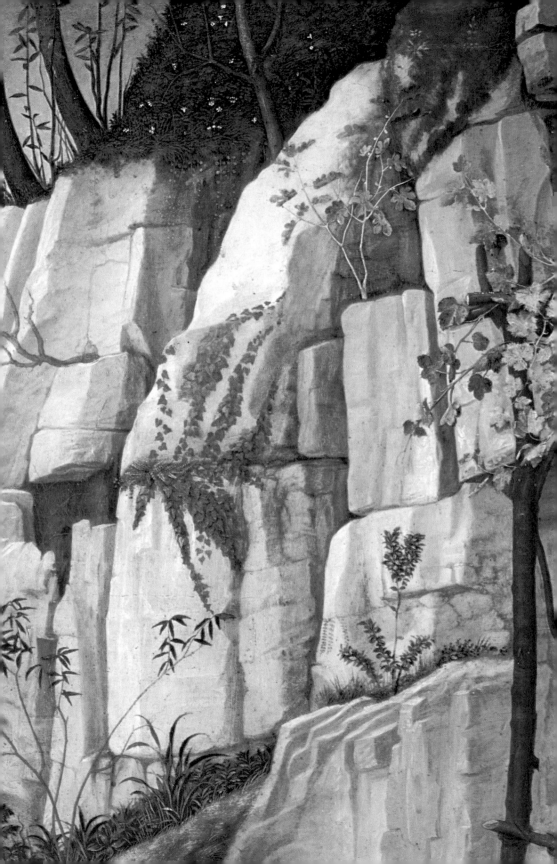

François Boucher, *Spring* (detail)

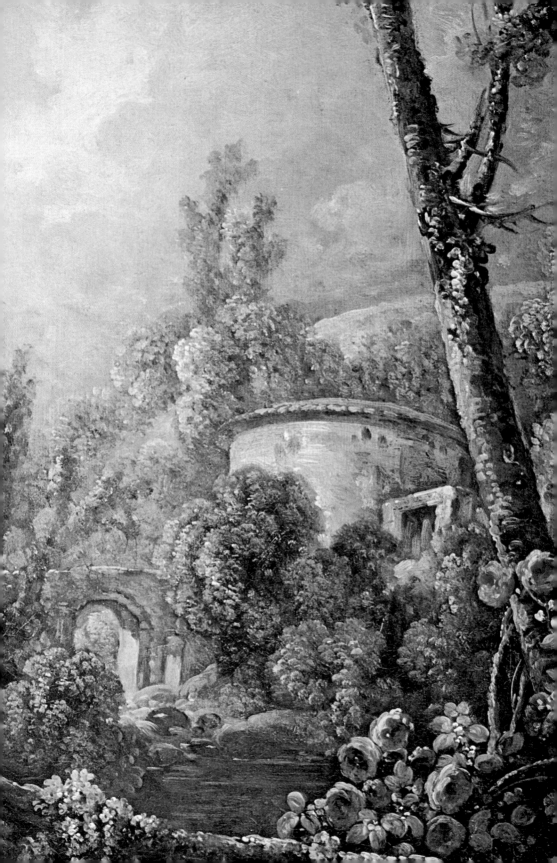

Agnolo Bronzino, *Lodovico Capponi* (detail)

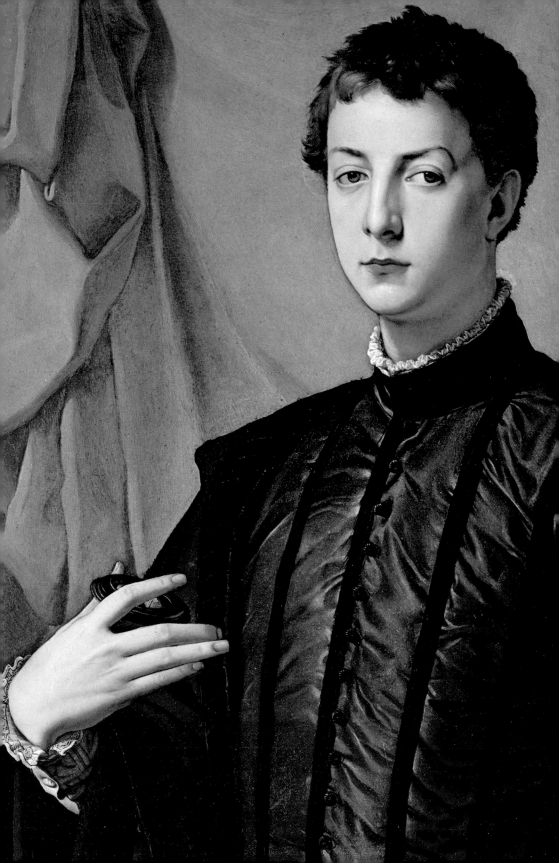

John Constable, *The White Horse* (detail)

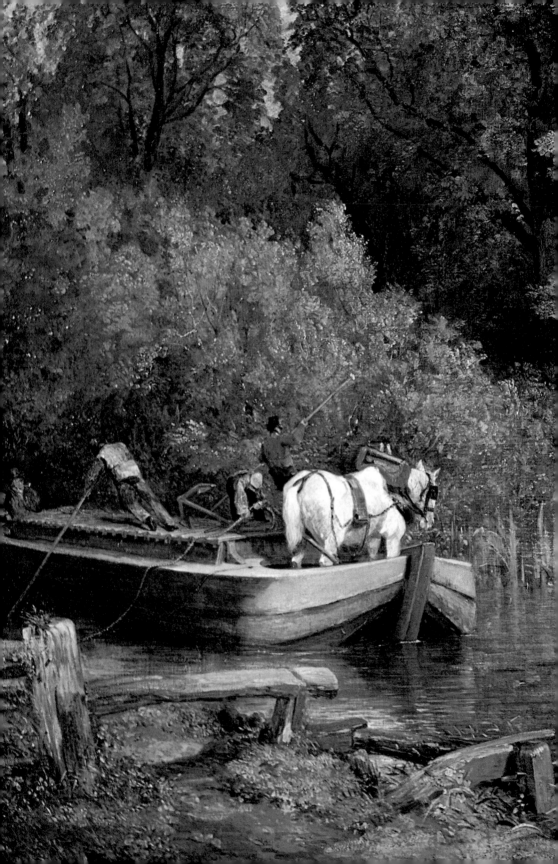

Gerard David, *The Deposition* (detail)

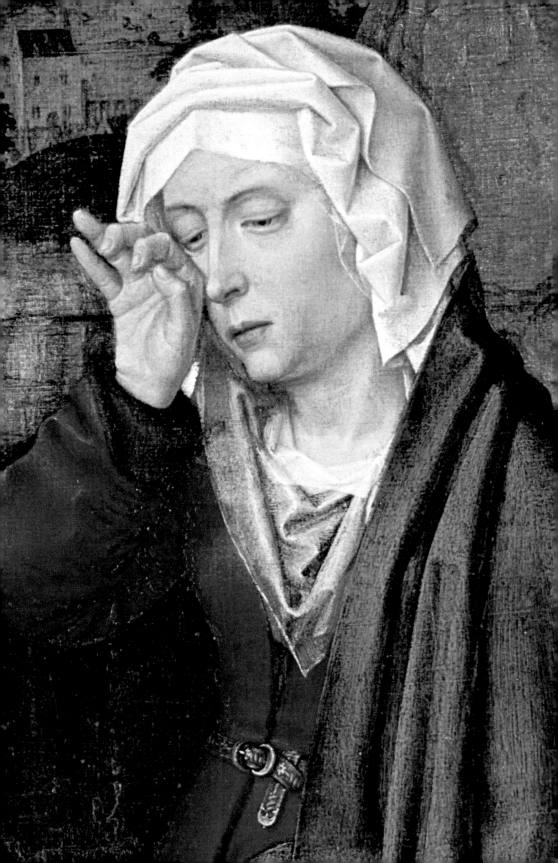

Jan van Eyck, *Virgin and Child, with Saints and Donor* (detail)

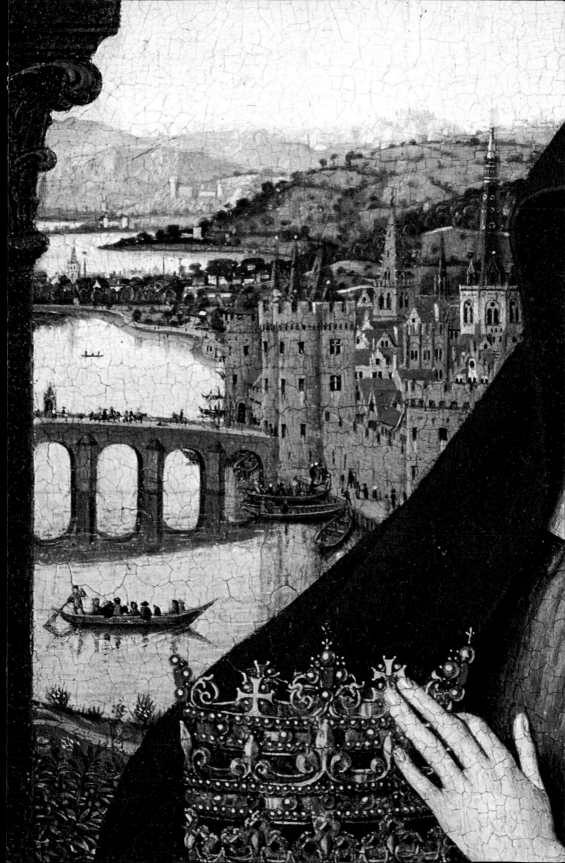

Thomas Gainsborough, *Sarah, Lady Innes* (detail)

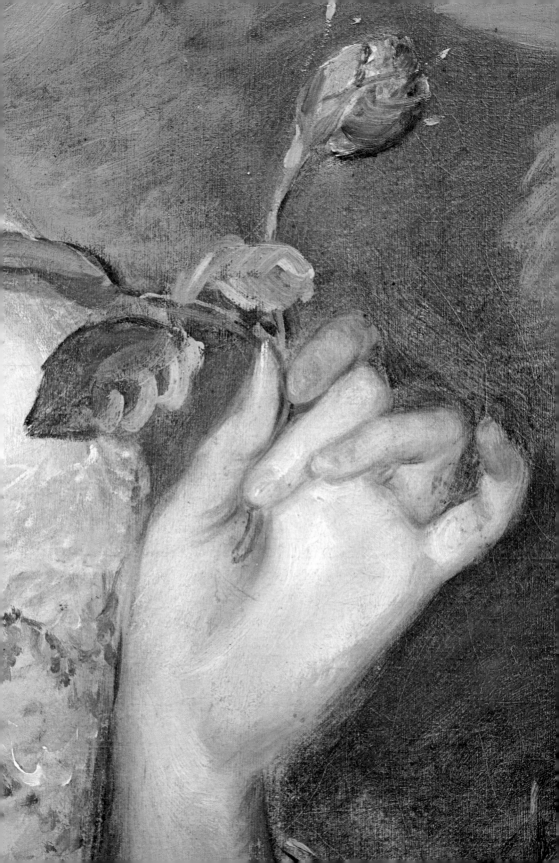

Rembrandt Harmensz. van Rijn, *Self-Portrait* (detail)